# THE FIXER

The Notorious Life of a
Front-Page Bail Bondsman

## IRA JUDELSON

### with Daniel Paisner

A TOUCHSTONE BOOK

PUBLISHED BY SIMON & SCHUSTER

NEW YORK   LONDON   TORONTO   SYDNEY   NEW DELHI

Touchstone
A Division of Simon & Schuster, Inc.
1230 Avenue of the Americas
New York, NY 10020

First Touchstone hardcover edition June 2014

For information about special discounts for bulk purchases,
please contact Simon & Schuster Special Sales at 1-866-506-1949
or business@simonandschuster.com.

The Simon & Schuster Speakers Bureau can bring authors to your live event.
For more information or to book an event, contact the Simon & Schuster Speakers Bureau at 1-866-248-3049 or visit our website at www.simonspeakers.com.

Jacket design by Ervin Serrano
Jacket photograph by Tom White

Manufactured in the United States of America

10  9  8  7  6  5  4  3  2  1

Library of Congress Cataloging-in-Publication Data
Judelson, Ira.
  The fixer : the notorious life of a front-page bail bondsman / Ira Judelson
with Daniel Paisner.
     pages   cm
  1. Judelson, Ira. 2.  Bail bond agents—New York (State)—Biography.
I.  Paisner, Daniel. II.  Title.
  HV8099.5.J83 2014
  345.747'056—dc23
  [B]
                    2013048578

ISBN 978-1-4516-9933-3
ISBN 978-1-4516-9935-7 (ebook)

To my wife, Blake,
who believed in me and stood by me when nobody else did

*A man of courage never needs weapons,*
*but he may need bail.*

—LEWIS MUMFORD

# CONTENTS

CONTENTS

# THE FIXER

# INTRODUCTION

## Who I Am

In Yiddish, a person who makes things happen is called a *macher*.

I grew up hearing that word, usually to describe a friend of the family who was a big shot, a fixer. Someone who could rattle a couple cages, bail you out of a jam. It's a term of respect, but it's almost like a grudging respect—like, if you don't blow a little smoke and show a little admiration, you'll never get the juice.

It helps to say the word out loud. You have to hear it to get its full meaning. You've got to go heavy on that *ch* sound in the middle—not like the *ch* at either end of *church*, but like the *ch* in *Chanukah*.

*Macher*. Like you've got something stuck in your throat.

It has no real equivalent in the English language, but it gets pretty damn close to what I do—what I do for a living and how I live my life, both. Guess you could say I make things happen. I know who to call, what buttons to push to open the right doors.

This doesn't begin to cover it, but it's a place to start.

So what do I do? I'm a bail bondsman—although this, too, only gets close to it. A lot of people, they hear that I'm a bail bondsman, their ears pick up. They don't have a clue what a bail bondsman is, what a bail bondsman does, but they think they have some idea from the movies, from television, from the nightly news. They think they know, but they don't really know.

I can't always explain it. The nuts and bolts—that's easy enough. But the day-to-day, the *essence*—that's tough to get across. So I tell them stories instead. For years, I've been telling stories. Every case comes with a story. Good guys. Bad guys. Mob guys. White-collar guys caught with their hands where their hands aren't supposed to be—I'd call it a cookie jar, but that makes it sound all sugar and spice, when in reality some of my clients are caught reaching into some dark, dark places. The stories I tell are not just about the transaction, the piece of business. They're not just about how I got this or that drug dealer out of jail. That's only a part of it. The rest of it, the *meat* of it, comes in how the characters around the courthouse go home with me at the end of each day. They're in my head, in my heart, to where I can't shake them.

Don't even bother to try.

My wife and kids, I can't shake them, either. They're tied into everything I do, every bond I write. It's like a package deal. I bring my work home with me, my cell's always within reach, but the calls cut both ways. It could be a defense attorney calling, middle of the night, asking me to bail out some superstar rapper or athlete before news of his arrest hits the papers. Or it could be one of my kids, pulling me from some judge's bench to tell me the dog shit on the rug.

Lately, I meet people, they want to know if I'm like Dog the Bounty Hunter, from that reality series. That's the knee-jerk response. They hear *bail bondsman*, they think "bounty hunter"—like the two go hand in hand. They think I chase fugitives for a living, but that's not it at all. Forget that the Dog Chapman approach just wouldn't cut it in New York. (Yeah, if I walked into the South Bronx waving a pellet gun, looking for some kid who jumped bail, I'd get *destroyed*.) And forget that bounties only come into play when someone jumps on me—meaning, when a client I've bailed out fails to turn up for a court date and forfeits his or her bond, leaving me on the hook.

I don't chase bad guys. They mostly come to me. Why? Because I lend them money at a rate. Because I'm their get-out-of-jail-free card—only it's not exactly free. They're still tied to the court, still in the system, still obligated to stand trial or work out some type of plea deal. Plus, they have to put up a house or a business or a piece of property as collateral. They have to pay me a fee. They have to promise not to skip town or duck out on a hearing. And with me, it's more than just a promise. It's like a blood oath, because if you fuck with me, you fuck with my living. You fuck with my family. It happens, but I don't like when it happens, so I do what I can to make sure it *doesn't* happen. Sometimes I make clients wear an ankle bracelet, or some other type of monitoring device, so I can keep tabs on them while we're waiting for their next court date to come around on the calendar. Sometimes all I can do is scare the plain crap out of them, tell them I'll jack up their family so hard they'll have no place to live, nothing in the bank.

I'm like a legal loan shark, what it comes down to. A *machor*

3

who steps in and finds a way to get suspects out from behind bars to wait out their trial dates at home, go about their business.

The bail bond business is one of the oldest professions on the planet—but not always the most honorable. I *get* that. The concept of bail goes all the way back to medieval times. I get *that,* too. The way it works is a judge sets a bail—a dollar amount, secured by cash or property—which is then pledged to a court to secure the release of a suspect from jail, pending a trial. On a misdemeanor—say, a breaking-and-entering charge, with no priors and no reason to think the defendant is a flight risk—bail could be as low as $500. On a felony—say, a rape or a murder charge, with a violent history and no good reason to stick around to stand trial—bail could run to seven figures. Or a judge could decide not to grant bail at all, for any reason at all. Up until 1984, pretrial detention was based solely on the risk of flight, but since then judges have had leeway to hold suspects charged with a crime of violence, drug offenses carrying maximum penalties of ten years or more, or in cases with the possibility of obstruction of justice or witness tampering.

It's a business of risk, basically. For the most part, the judge has to weigh the severity of the crime and the danger to society a suspect might pose on the streets against the presumption of flight risk. On my end, I have to consider the size of the bond against whatever cash or jewelry or property my client is able to put up as collateral, and then I weigh *that* against my own thoughts on whether that person is going anywhere.

Basically, you don't want to need to call me—but I'm a good guy to have on your side if you do. I don't give a shit if you're innocent. That's not my problem. I don't give a shit about the mistakes you might have made in your past—just the ones you might make next. Only thing I care about is that you don't screw me over and take the roof over my head. If I trust you, I'll go to the wall for you. But I need something back in the bargain. I need to know you'll be good to your word.

And here's the thing: if I trust you, I'll do you an extra solid. I might be the only person keeping you from getting sucked up in *the injustice system*. Think of it: you're locked up in Rikers, with no protection and a pretty face—who the hell else you gonna call? I know who to touch for a favor to make sure your time inside goes easy. I know which judges might let you slide and which ones have zero tolerance. I have a direct line to white-shoe lawyers who'll work pro bono for the right case, and I know the cops and the DAs who believe in second chances.

So, yeah . . . I guess I'm a *macher*. I know people. It's my job to make things happen, even when they're not supposed to happen. It's my job to get you out of jail—and then, if it works out you have to go back in, to make sure you're protected. I've helped enough pimps, hustlers, and gangbangers to where there's always someone I can call.

I've got more favors coming back to me than I know what to do with—might as well put 'em to work, right?

# 1

# The Fixer

So let's see what a day in these murky waters looks like—one day in particular.

I got a call from a lawyer I hadn't worked with before: "Mr. Judelson, I have a fifty-thousand-dollar bond I need to get done. Wondering if you're available."

"Sure," I said. "I'm always available. What's the case?"

"Not your usual. A young man who warranted." Meaning, a kid who'd already jumped a bond—not the best quality in a potential client.

I cut the lawyer off right there: "I'm not doing the bail." The last thing I need is to get involved with a kid who's a proven flight risk. I learned this the hard way—like, a couple times over.

But the lawyer kept at it. "Please. All due respect. Just hear me out."

So I heard him out. A young man, let's call him Peter—for Peter Parker, natch—was at a club a couple years back with his girlfriend. They were in a mosh-pit-type setting, together with a group of friends and a whole bunch of people they didn't know. Someone said something or did something disrespectful to Peter's girlfriend, so Peter and another friend roughed the guy up a bit.

That would have been the end of it except for a couple details. One, the guy they roughed up was the son of a New York City detective. And two, a fight like this, two versus one, was no longer considered a simple assault in New York State. Now it went down as a gang assault, which was a whole other ball game.

The cops arrested Peter and his buddy. Worked them over pretty good. Told them they'd get fucked in the ass and hurt in every which way on the inside—not just by the cons but by the corrections officers. Scared the crap out of these kids, which is what happens when you mess with the son of a New York City detective. Peter got out on a $10,000 cash bail and immediately bolted to Seattle. His buddy went to trial and was acquitted. Eventually, Peter was picked up for running a red light and was sent back to New York by the State of Washington on a warrant, and now they were charging him with bail jumping on top of the gang assault.

All of this was problem enough, but there was an even bigger problem—Peter was a serious Spider-Man fan. He had webs tattooed on his chest and arms, the name Peter Parker tattooed across his chest. He was like one of these fanatics you see at comic book conventions, caught between fantasy and reality, only here the kid's fascination put him in deep, deep shit. The reason? In prison, web tattoos put it out there that you're a white supremacist—not the kind of calling card you want if you're looking to do your time unnoticed. Since he was brought back to New York, Peter had been beaten daily by the Latin Kings, the Bloods, the Crips . . . and all but left for dead, so the lawyer was pushing for a plea and a six-week "stay" to give the kid time to have the tattoos removed.

The kid wouldn't last if he was sent upstate. Not looking like *that*.

"He's a simple kid in a bad spot," the lawyer said. "Got almost a childlike mentality. He didn't get the webs because he's a supremacist. He got the webs because he likes Spider-Man."

I took the case.

Wasn't a lot of money. The mother was a single mom. An older brother would put up collateral for the bond, but most of that had come from a settlement in a car accident. Once I looked at the whole deal, I didn't think Peter was any kind of flight risk, so I wasn't too concerned about the numbers—but that was just me. The judge, though, he wanted some assurances that this kid would stick around all six weeks.

As part of the agreement, Peter would have to wear a monitoring device on his ankle, which he'd have to pay for, so I prevailed on the ankle-bracelet company to go easy on the fee—said, "Do the right thing here. He'll only be on it six weeks. Family's got no money. Kid's already had it rougher than rough."

The day we got him out, the kid's eyes were swollen shut. He looked like he'd been run over—twice.

I knew this kid was going through hell. It made me sick to my stomach. All he'd done was pop this cop's kid in the face. His running buddy that night at the club had already been acquit ted, but because Peter had jumped, he was now looking at one to three years on the gang-assault charge, with another one to three years on the bail-jumping charge, to run consecutively. All told, he could have been looking at four or five years—an insane stretch for what should have been a nothing violation.

At first, I'd thought this lawyer was doing a good and creative job for his client, recognizing this unique situation with the spiderweb tattoos and moving to set things right, but the more I talked with Peter and his mother, the more I realized the guy was just a hack. I don't like to hate on a hardworking defense lawyer, especially since I need all the friends I can get to build up my referrals, but this guy sounded like the poster boy for half-assedness.

I got the mother alone and started pumping her with questions. Learned she'd paid the attorney a $15,000 retainer, and that her son had already been at Rikers for eight weeks, so it's not like this lawyer was moving with any kind of haste. Plus, the lawyer had convinced these people to take a plea—to what was essentially the top charge, on the long end of the recommended sentence.

Best I could tell, all this guy had done was pocket his fee, twiddle his thumbs, and call me in to do the bail.

Next morning, I called the ADA—the assistant district attorney—on the case, a guy I'd known for years. He had just returned to the DA's office after a stint in the private sector, so we spent a couple minutes catching up, comparing notes, but then I switched gears and started talking about the case—said, "What are you doing with this kid?"

"Ira," he said, sensing I was more than just asking here, "he's taking a plea. It's a done deal."

"You shittin' me?" I shot back. "You're really charging him with a C felony?" Meaning, the kind of violent crime that earns you time upstate, instead of a simple assault, a Class D felony, where you might only do city time.

"He pled to it," the ADA said, starting to get his back up.

I wasn't ready to let it go. "Come on. This wasn't a cop's kid, what would the charge be? Might even be a fuckin' misdemeanor."

We went back and forth and all around, got nowhere. Finally, the prosecuting attorney tried to shut me up—said, "Be a bondsman, Ira." Like he was putting me in my place.

He didn't want to hear from me on this, it was clear.

I brought the case home with me. A lot of these cases, they come home with me. Stayed up late all that night talking to my wife, Blake, running through all these different scenarios. "Blake, he's gonna get killed upstate."

"Yeah," she said, "but he did run."

"He's not a bad kid," I said, getting all worked up again. "He's just in a bad spot. Wrong place, wrong time, wrong people. He ran because these cops put the fear of God into him."

Next morning, I got the mother back on the phone, asked her where she'd found her son's attorney.

"On the computer," she said.

"What about a court-appointed attorney? Anybody ever talk to you about going that route?"

"On the computer is better. Private is better."

This poor woman didn't know how to advocate for her son, so I called the shit attorney and said, "Just curious, how'd you get my name?"

He gave me the name of a lawyer I knew, so I called the lawyer I knew and filled him in. I thanked him for the referral, then told him how this attorney had taken a $15,000 retainer and basically sold out the kid, made one nothing court appearance, hadn't even broken a sweat.

The lawyer I knew said, "What do you want from me, Ira? I just sent you some business. That's all."

"I want you to call your friend, get him to take back the plea."

He kind of snorted, as if to say, *Yeah, like that's gonna happen.*

Next, I called back the ADA, left a message, thought there was a good chance he wouldn't even call me back—not after the way our last call had gone. But I did hear back from him, an hour or so later, so I told him to let this lawyer get his plea back.

The ADA said, "Ira, I'm gonna say this to you one more time. Be a bondsman. It's not up to me to tell this kid's lawyer how to do his job."

"Understood, but you're doing the wrong thing here."

"Kid's pleading to the charge. There is no wrong thing here." Then he hung up. Two hours later, he called back. "Have the attorney file a motion to withdraw the plea, with nonopposition from the DA. I'll let him plea to a D, a simple assault."

"What's he get out of that?" I asked.

"He'll do a year."

"You're doing a great thing here."

"Fuck you, Ira." Then he hung up again.

Going from a C to a D like that, it was huge—wasn't everything, but it meant this kid might be able to stay at Rikers, where we might be able to arrange some sort of protective custody. His prospects went from grim to not-so-fucking grim, just on the back of this one small act of humanity.

But first I had to set the damn deal in motion. I called the hack. "You ever hear of a motion to withdraw, with nonopposition from the DA?"

"Sure, that's when the judge authorizes me to take back my plea," he said.

"Why don't you do that?"

"I'm not following you, why would I do that?"

"Because the DA will go along with it."

"No way the DA goes along with it." Like he had a read on the situation instead of no fucking clue.

"I'm telling you, file this motion. The DA will go along with it."

I could hear the guy getting more and more anxious on the other end of the phone, like it was some sort of affront to his profession, me telling him what to do. He said, "Who the hell do you think you are? I brought you in on this."

"You brought me in on this? You're taking fifteen thousand dollars from these people. You went to court once. This kid's been beaten half to fuckin' death, and all you've done is plea him to the fuckin' charge. For the full fuckin' sentence. Just so you can get this off your calendar."

Things went downhill from here, and for the second time in under an hour an attorney told me to fuck off and hung up on me.

But this guy must have heard me, or maybe somebody else talked to somebody else, because four weeks later Peter was back in court, withdrawing his plea. He looked like he'd lost a ton of weight. His bruises had started to heal, but the tattoos were a problem. He'd been to a couple tattoo-removal experts, but the best these people could do was make them darker, unrecognizable. The kid was still all tatted up, but you couldn't tell they were webs, so he was good on that score at least.

And the ADA was good to his word. He let the attorney take back his plea and cop to a simple assault. Peter wound up finishing his bid at Rikers, in protective custody, and he was still screwed in all kinds of wrong ways . . . but it could have been worse. It could have been way fucking worse.

Another day in particular.

A female teacher in Brooklyn, thirtysomething, charged with having sex with a minor, a sixteen-year-old student. Kid was a football player. According to the charges, they'd had sex in the teacher's office at school, in an SUV parked outside the kid's house, in the teacher's house. There was a "paper" trail of over three thousand text messages.

No getting away from this one.

The complaint came from the kid's ex-girlfriend. The kid denied it at first, but then the detectives pushed up on him, showed him the phone records, told him there were eyewitnesses. Plus, the kid had his chest out. He'd been bragging to his teammates—basically, telling anyone who'd listen.

*Hey, I'm fucking my teacher.*

Like it was a big deal.

The call came from the teacher's husband—an attorney who mostly worked guardianships, trusts. "Ira, man, how you doin'? I've got to arrange bail for my wife." Like he'd known me for a hundred years.

I listened and kept thinking what this poor husband was dealing with. His wife brings this kind of shame on his house, on his marriage, it's all over the tabloids, and all he could do was work the phones, try to make things easy for her.

The shit some people are forced to slog through, the choices they make when they're up against it . . . it was in my face every damn day and it never stopped surprising me.

The husband told me his wife had been assigned a teachers' union lawyer to handle her arraignment. He gave me the name. I told him I'd never heard of her, which was not exactly true. "She's sending us to another bail bondsman," he said. "Every attorney I know, they say I should use you, but this union lawyer, she's sending us to this other guy."

From his voice, I got that he was on top of things, wanted to do the right thing, but underneath he sounded beaten, whipped. Like he'd rather be doing just about anything else than arranging bail for his adulterous wife—his *scandalously* adulterous wife. It had to be humiliating, infuriating.

I said, "Listen, I don't want to get into a pissing contest. You know who I am. Your friends, these other lawyers, they know who I am."

Truth was, it didn't much matter who wrote this teacher's bond. A bail up to $50,000, any licensed bondsman could do the job. It only gets complicated when it gets complicated—like, when there's a surety hearing, and the district attorney wants to know who's putting up what piece of property to secure the bond. Bottom line, judges want to know where the money is coming from, and the more money's involved, the more documentation they need. Also, the bigger the headlines, the more attention gets paid to these kinds of details, so it starts to matter.

No way to know just yet what kind of number we were looking at for bail, but I didn't think it'd be huge. Probably $50,000 . . . $75,000 . . . somewhere in there. I didn't say anything to this lawyer husband, but it felt to me like his wife had a deal going with another bondsman. That's how it goes. A lot of bondsmen give kickbacks to lawyers for sending them clients, but I show my appreciation in other ways. You send me a bunch of business, I'll send you to see *Rock of Ages*, *Jersey Boys*, whatever's big, whatever's a tough ticket. I've got Yankee seats, Ranger seats, a table at Rao's. The lawyers I work with, I give to all their charities. I'll send them over a nice case of wine, something.

This guy, he decided to go against his wife's lawyer. Kickback or no, he wanted to call his own shots, so he came by my office the next day, a Thursday. He said if the bail was low, he'd put it up on a credit card. If it was high, he'd use his brother-in-law's house as collateral.

Either way, it was fine by me.

A lot of folks, these kinds of circumstances, they wonder why they need me. If they have the money, the collateral, they figure they can post the bail on their own, save themselves my percentage, but that's not how it works. The court won't let you put up your house directly, it's got to flow through a licensed bondsman, so I told the husband what he already knew. Told him his wife wouldn't be arraigned until the next day, maybe not until after the weekend, and he was okay with that. I got that he was pissed, a little—not at me, but at the situation. At his wife. Don't think it mattered to him too much if she stayed in custody another day or two. I mean, they had her for messing around with this high school kid, they had these three thousand text messages, his life was plastered on the pages of the *Post*. That had to be tough—so maybe he was thinking a little payback, a little time inside, wasn't the worst thing in the world.

That night, six thirty or so, I was coaching my kid's Little League team, trying to squeeze a couple hours of normal into my crazy day. Our team was the Long Island Orthopedics—not the most menacing team name in the league, I'll give you that. I'd wanted to sponsor the team myself—Judelson Bail Bonds, has a nice ring to it—but the league organizers didn't think this was such a good idea, and when I pointed out it would be like the Chico's Bail Bonds team from the *Bad News Bears* movies, they still didn't think it was such a good idea, so now we were the fightin' Orthopedics. It rubbed me wrong. I'd wanted to do right by our community, give back a couple dollars and sponsor my own kid's team, but the folks who run the town think there's a negative to what I do. Bail bonds? Either they don't get it, and they're afraid of the association—or they do, and they're even more afraid, which in some ways is worse.

We had the field from six to seven thirty, and I wanted to make good use of our limited practice time. Two other dads with sons on the team, they helped me out with the coaching, so we had the kids split up, doing different drills. Coaching youth baseball, there can be a lot of waiting around, so we tried to have two or three things going on at a time to cut down on all that standing still—and usually, it worked out pretty well.

On this night, though, I was pulled away by my cell phone. My wife is on me about this all the time, but my big worry is, if the phone rings and I'm not there to answer it, they'll just call someone else. That's the nature of the bail bond business. Folks want out when they want out. They want help when they want help. They don't want to wait around for me to finish dinner with my family, for me to get done teaching these kids how to hit the cutoff man, for me to sit down at my desk first thing in the morning and start returning calls.

They think to call me, I should be available to answer the phone.

Anyway, practice kind of came to a halt as I waved to one of my assistant coaches to take over for me so I could slink behind the fence and flip open my phone. A court officer I knew in Manhattan was calling, and at first I couldn't think why.

"Hey, Ira, you working this teacher case out in Brooklyn? The one supposedly having an affair with a student?"

I was half-listening, half-paying attention to the drill I'd abandoned on the field. "Yeah. How'd you hear about that?"

Before the guy could answer, I put my phone to my chest and shouted out a reminder to my son, Casey, telling him to crow-hop on his throws back to the infield—something we'd been working on, a way for him to put a little extra something on the ball.

Turned out this court officer was married to the union attorney assigned to represent the teacher. I'd had no idea. I heard that and thought, Small world. And it is—only in the small world of New York's criminal justice system this means you've got to be careful how you play it. Everyone knows everyone else. Every move can come back to bite you on the ass or kiss you full on the mouth. Like here: I take a case, guy comes into my office to sign the papers in the afternoon, end of the day the whole city knows about it.

Still, I couldn't think why this guy was calling, so I played dumb. "What can I do for you?"

"My wife, she's worried about this case. We're supposed to leave town for a couple days, on vacation, but she doesn't want to lose this client." So he was calling to see if his wife was about to get pushed off the case, and to see if he needed to smooth things over with me. He didn't say as much, but he was fishing. He knew the husband had been to see me.

"You asking me if the teacher is looking for another attorney?" I said.

"Yeah. Guess that's what I'm asking."

So I laid it out for him. "If I had to bet, I'd say this teacher's gonna use your wife as an arraignment attorney because she's covered by the union. But that's only for now."

We went back and forth for a while—him, angling for some kind of inside track, asking if I could put in a good word; me, thinking how to tell this guy I knew his wife was sending business to my competitors. This, after his wife and I had worked together in the past, so it's not like she didn't know me from any other bondsman in the phone book. Here was this correction officer reaching out for a favor, for information, and here I was sitting with this trump card, wondering when to play it. Knowing it'll make the favor twice as big, the information twice as valuable. Finally, I just came out with it: "The thing is, your wife is telling the teacher and her husband to use a different bail company."

The correction officer didn't say anything. For a beat, I wondered if the line had gone dead, but then he started to talk. "About that," he said. "That's probably my fault. I'm the one who knows you. Probably, I didn't do such a good job letting my wife know you're the guy to see."

"Don't worry about it," I said, trying to walk the high road, leaving the door open on our doing business in the future.

"No, you should know. It's on me. My wife, she works with a bondsman one week, that's the guy she recommends the next week. She doesn't always pay attention."

I left this alone because I thought I'd made my point. I knew if I found a way to keep this guy's wife in the picture, I'd be the first guy her clients called, here on in.

The whole time we were talking, I kept setting the phone down to coach one of my kids on the field—reminding this one, little, guy to stay low on a ground ball, to keep his body in front. I was only half-listening to this court officer, reaching out on behalf of his lawyer wife, only half-following what was going on with the fightin' Orthopedics, trying to get ready for a big game on Saturday. I hated that I was spread so thin, but this was nothing new. Everything's up in the air with me. I'm constantly juggling a million things. The trick, always, is to keep any one thing from crashing to the ground.

At least, that's the idea.

I turned my attention back to the phone call, to this husband. "Tell you what. We get through the arraignment, I'll get with the teacher, maybe with her husband, I'll tell them it makes sense to stay the course with your wife. I'll tell them they're in good hands."

"That's decent of you, Ira." He wasn't expecting this—not after the way I'd busted his hump about his wife's referrals. I was playing three sides against the middle, but we both knew the drill.

"Don't worry about it," I said. "Works out for both of us. I put in a good word for your wife, she puts in a good word for me down the road."

Next morning, I got to the courthouse in Brooklyn before noon. The place was packed with reporters, rubberneckers. Roseanne Colletti was there, from Channel 4, WNBC-TV. Juliet Papa, from 1010 WINS. John Slattery, from Channel 2, WCBS-TV. Reporters from all the local newspapers. It's like I had to run a gauntlet on the way in, everybody shouting at me:

*Hey, Ira, can I get a few minutes?*

*Ira, I need a statement.*

*What do you think about this judge, Ira?*

The usual.

The husband was waiting for me inside. He was wearing a colorful old suit—and along with his wild, Fu Manchu–type mustache, he seemed pretty out of place. Our eyes met.

I walked over to him. "How's it going, man? You holding up?"

"What can I tell you?"

I liked this guy, wanted things to go well for him. "Let's hope the bail's low."

"Yeah. Save my money for a divorce lawyer."

He made a lot of jokes like this. *Someday, when I'm single, maybe we'll go grab a beer.* Like that. They were more jabs than jokes.

The judge read the charges against my client. Child molestation, endangering the welfare of a minor, and on and on—a long list, but there was no statutory rape charge because they couldn't prove the sexual intercourse, not yet.

The DA asked for a $50,000 bond, then detailed how my client had performed oral sex on this kid football player in his bedroom, with more than a dozen sexual liaisons, and I kept looking over at the husband, his head in his hands, this ashen look on his face. I put my hand on his hand. It was something to do, some way to tell this guy I knew he was hurting, listening to all this shit about his wife.

Hard not to like this guy, feel for him.

Finally, after the DA made his case and the union lawyer made her case for the teacher, the judge set bail at $10,000. I was surprised at the low number—glad for the husband, who now didn't have to dig too, too deep to save his wife's ass; not so glad for me, because it meant my fee would also be low, since it's done by percentage.

We got through what we had to get through, and at the other

end there was a whole other gauntlet on the way out of the court-room. The same reporters, asking the same questions.

*How's the husband, Ira?*

*What did she use to secure the bail?*

*Where will she go from here?*

I'm thinking, How the hell do I know where this teacher goes from here? How do they *think* the husband is doing? But all I could say was that this was a difficult time for this family, that I didn't believe my client was a flight risk, that I would have written this bail up to any amount the judge asked.

As I left, I caught a glimpse of my client, the teacher. We hadn't spoken yet—all of my dealings had been with her husband. But here I was up close enough to look right into her eyes, and they came back blank. It was almost creepy, the empty stare that bounced off this woman. I didn't know if she was in shock, or on some type of medication, or if she'd just completely shut down. But then I caught myself and thought, Maybe this is the only way to get through something like this. Maybe if you're a teacher and you step out with a sixteen-year-old student and get caught in such a public, flagrant way, the only thing to do is shut down.

Soon as I could, I broke for my car, where my right-hand man, Damon Romanelli, was waiting. My buddy. I'd known Damon since just about forever; he was a couple years ahead of me in high school, and he's become one of my closest friends. Guy's been through some rough patches, but these days he's doing okay. He works for me, collects money for me, watches my back. Some people in this business, they call a guy like Damon their muscle, but with me it's way more than that. He's my muscle, my head, my heart. He's got my back—and he knows his shit. Spent ten years in jail—first for an armored car heist and later on for attempted

22

murder. He's an ex-Marine, he knows how things go in the joint, on the street, all over, and I can't imagine doing what I do without Damon at my side.

Plus, I like having him around.

As I slipped into the car, Damon asked how things went in court, but before I could tell him, my phone started vibrating. First it was the union attorney thanking me for my help. Then it was the husband thanking me for my support, making another half joke about how he would soon be single. Then it was Laura Italiano from the *Post*, looking for a comment. After that, Roseanne Colletti asked me to call if anything broke on this case.

Between calls, Damon and I talked, listened to the radio. The usual bullshit. Soon, 1010 WINS had a bulletin, Juliet Papa giving her report, and there I was, coming through the car speakers, talking about the case.

Damon heard me on the radio and started laughing. "Ira, man, this is fuckin' sick."

And it was. It *is*. We were used to it by now, but Damon's right—it *was* completely sick, this swirl of attention, this media circus, me in the middle.

Me, of all people . . .

# 2

# Story of My Life

I didn't exactly grow up wanting to be a bail bondsman—but I did know what a bail bondsman was.

I used to hear plenty of stories about guys who were serving at Rikers from my father, who was a teacher there. Guess it was a little strange, looking back—me as a kid, knowing what it meant for someone to do time at a place like Rikers. To understand what it was like *inside* for a lot of these guys. In my neighborhood, most kids didn't know shit about prison life, other than what they saw in the movies, on television. It wasn't real to them, but it was real to me. Wasn't anything I was interested in, in my own life, but it was in the air and all around—kind of like the background music of my childhood.

Sports—that was more my thing. I wanted to be a professional ballplayer. Baseball, football . . . I was good at both. Even had a shot at a football scholarship at Columbia if I could have gotten my SAT scores within spitting distance of a halfway decent number. Academically, though, I couldn't get out of my own way. I learned in high school that I had ADD, attention deficit disorder, something it would have been nice to know *way* before I was sixteen. I remember hearing this diagnosis and being so completely pissed. At my parents, at my teachers, at the world. Those three little letters, ADD, explained away all my struggles, but they found me too late to make any kind of difference. No resource room, no extra help . . . none of that. Only way I'd gotten through some of my classes was by cheating and conniving and sweet-talking. I'd been a star athlete all through high school, so that helped. I was all-state and all-county in football and baseball, all-conference in basketball, and when you can hit and run and jump and tackle, your teachers tend to look the other way and leave you alone. I didn't know enough to notice, or to mind. I was passed along from one grade to the next, thinking school was the same tough slog for everyone else.

I couldn't get my scores anywhere close to what I needed to land that Columbia scholarship; ended up going to a bunch of different colleges. Didn't last too long at any one of them: community college to get my grades up, Cortland to play football, Iona to finally finish things out.

I could probably have stayed at Cortland and had a decent college career, Division III, but I got homesick after just a week or so. Plus, my mom was in and out of the hospital, struggling with breast cancer, so I turned tail and headed home. In terms of football, I should have stuck it out. In just that first week of preseason, I'd worked my way up from sixth or seventh on the coach's depth chart, playing safety, to first or second, so I had that going for me, but the tug of home was powerful. I was a mama's boy, I guess—that, and I felt out of my element. Not on the football field, I had that part down, but in the classroom, on campus, everywhere else. I was always looking for angles and ways to cut corners.

I just wanted to get out and get on with it.

This left me pretty much unprepared for whatever came next. I was no closer to any kind of goal, or even any kind of starting line. Yet, by some sick string of miracles, I'd got my college degree, but I hadn't *learned* anything, other than how to get through college. I had no interests, no talents, outside of sports. I certainly had no training in any kind of field or discipline, so I bounced around for a while, kept throwing opportunities against the wall, hoping something might stick.

I didn't have a head for business, but I couldn't see myself in any kind of traditional job. Sitting at a desk, pushing papers around, going to meetings, sucking up to a boss . . . it was like nails on a chalkboard to me. Something to be avoided at all costs—or for as long as possible. By default, I started thinking like an entrepreneur, figured I could be in business for myself, do my own thing. Wasn't the best fit for me just then. Didn't exactly match with my skill set—but that was mostly because I didn't have a skill set, just a set notion of what I *didn't* want to do.

So what do you do when you're up against it? When you can't think of anything else to do? You look to start your own business, but my entrepreneurial streak only took me so far. I was in the gym business for a stretch, started out well enough, but then my partner stole from me and I was back where I started. (Story of my young life—part one.) I bought and operated a couple nightclubs in the Carolinas, and they started to throw off some money . . . until those businesses went bad, too. (Story of my young life—part two.)

For a while in there, I went in with a buddy on a sports agency, thinking we'd be like Jerry Maguire and conquer the big-time sports world. Trouble was, we needed clients, and it wasn't such an easy sell, getting these young athletes to go with us when we hadn't done a lick of business. That didn't stop us, though. We were determined. We started traveling up and down the East Coast, trying to sign up-and-coming college athletes to our firm—football and baseball players, mostly, because that was what we knew. Spent a lot of time hanging around frat houses and field houses, which in retrospect was kind of creepy, but it was the best way we could think to troll for student-athletes in need of representation. Also, it was a good excuse for me to keep drinking and roughhousing and generally goofing off, same way I'd done all through college. (Story of my young life—parts three and four, because I kept at this one for a good long while, thought it might amount to something.)

We managed to land a half dozen or so clients, but nobody at the A-level, no budding superstars, just good, solid, knockaround athletes who might get a shot. A couple times, we'd get a relationship going with a kid who seemed like he might get chosen in one of the early rounds of the NFL draft, and we'd go back and forth with him and his family, set him up with a cell phone, run a tab for him and his friends at one of our bars, do whatever we could to bring him on board, and then at the very end he'd call us and say he decided to sign with IMG or one of the other big-time agencies. Closest thing we had to a real payday was when one of our guys signed with the New England Patriots, but he got cut by the end of his first preseason camp, so that was that.

I was a hustler. Wasn't something I'd learned in any kind of academic way, although I guess you could say I picked it up in school, hustling to skate by. Wasn't something I'd learned from my parents, was just part of my personality, only it wasn't doing me any good, not at first. I see now that I was banking a lot of the skills I'd need one day in the bond business—learning how to read people, how not to take no for an answer, how to think for myself and get out in front of a piece of trouble. I wasn't quite there yet. Wasn't quite ready to do anything but tread some serious water. I mean, it's one thing to talk a good game—I had that part *down*—but it's something else to turn that talk into something real, something viable, and I was having a little trouble on that turn.

Got to where I moved back home with my parents, just to catch my breath, only the change of scenery didn't help. Yeah, I'd cut down on my expenses, but now I had a cap on my prospects, too. I became depressed—not clinically depressed, but I was in a deep, black funk, couldn't see a way to get myself going on any positive path. I started sleeping until one or two o'clock in the afternoons, grabbing at odd jobs just to keep a little walking-around money in my pockets. Some days, there was no good reason to get out of bed. I worked as a bouncer in a couple local bars. I hauled fish at the Fulton Street Market. The worst was a gig gluing fake labels on the backs of illegal pharmaceutical products that some guys I knew were reselling to CVS. I'd get $100 in cash for each shift, and I'd be working alongside three or four illegal Mexican immigrants thinking, So this is it for me, huh? This is why I went to college?

From there, things went from bad to worse. They repo-ed my car, a sweet Ford Bronco with lease payments I couldn't handle, so then I had to borrow my dad's car whenever I needed to go out. Once, I asked this girl on a date, and when we got to the movies, I pulled out my wallet and saw I didn't have any money, so I did what any self-respecting young man would do: I bailed—ducked into the theater on some excuse or other, then disappeared out the back door.

I was going nowhere, in no kind of hurry. And the worst part was I didn't see any way up or out of my situation.

I didn't hit bottom until one Halloween night when I was twenty-eight years old. I'd been living with my parents for a few years, hadn't earned or saved enough to even think about moving out on my own, and I went to answer the door and give out some candy to little kids. It was something to do to kill the time before I could go out drinking with my buddies, but when I opened the door, there was my ex-girlfriend from high school, with her three kids, all dressed up for trick-or-treating. She couldn't have been nicer, or happier to see me—or, at least, she couldn't have pretended any better—but I was humiliated.

She said, "Ira! So good to see you! I didn't know you were back in town."

I lied, "Yeah, I'm just back for a couple days. Helping out my folks with a couple things."

She asked if I was going to our ten-year high school reunion, which was coming up in a couple weeks. I hadn't even realized it'd been ten years since we graduated. On the one hand, it felt like just yesterday when I was kicking butt on the field and chasing girls who made themselves pretty damn easy to catch, but on the other hand it felt like forever. I tried to remember what it was like to have my whole life stretching out before me, to have the feeling that anything was possible, that I was invincible. I hadn't felt that way in a long, long time, and it took seeing my ex-girlfriend having her life together, married, with three kids, for me to see the kind of shit I was in.

Out of this low moment, I told myself, good things would happen.

I continued to be Charlie Hustle, but now I was desperate to get my shit together. I had no clear idea what kind of career I was chasing, but I was looking for a better way forward. At the same time, I started playing more and more softball—competitive, top-tier softball. Bet you didn't know there was such a thing, huh? Frankly, I didn't either, but I'd started playing with some good teams, and some of the tournaments we entered offered big-time prize money to the winners. So, with nothing else going on, I talked myself into believing I was some kind of professional athlete. I even said this to people—out loud!—like it sounded impressive.

Anyway, softball was a way to fill the time, a place to put my focus. Looking back, though, I think the game was part of the same chase—a way to jump-start my life. This was me trying to reach back to a time when I had the world licked on the ball field, trying to regain whatever confidence I'd had as a ballplayer. I was on a team sponsored by a big criminal defense lawyer. He put together this dream team of softball players, and he bankrolled us in tournaments all over the country. Wasn't any kind of big deal to him—just something he enjoyed doing. It was like his hobby, his golf, his Lamborghini. Vegas, Florida, North Carolina . . . some of them with a prize for the first-place team, but mostly it was about bragging rights on the softball circuit. He paid our way, covered our expenses on the road, and in some cases threw us a per game salary of $25 or $50—with a sweet bonus tacked on when we won a big tournament.

One afternoon, leading up to a road trip, I stopped by our sponsor's office to pick up my airline ticket, together with whatever spending money I might need to make my way out to wherever we were going. You have to realize, I was living from odd job to odd job, so even this walking-around money was significant. I'd be away at a tournament trying to eat off the dollar menu at McDonald's so I could pocket some of my per diem, that's how strapped I was for cash.

When I got to the defense attorney's office, he was meeting with a client—a young Hispanic male—and I sat outside the office door, waiting for a good time to poke my head inside. I didn't need an appointment, but I didn't want to interrupt. The door was open, so I could hear the whole conversation between our sponsor and his client. I'd arrived in the middle of a heated exchange—something to do with the client's getting his mother's house back, along with some other thing about doing five years down.

At this point, I walked into our sponsor's office. He was cool, kept an open-door policy with his softball guys, didn't seem to mind if we drifted in and out of his business, even when our drifting in and out stepped a little bit on his attorney-client privilege. Plus, I'd watched enough cop shows, courtroom shows, to piece together what was going on, and I wanted to get this Hispanic guy's take. Something about his story just struck me, you know, and I started pumping him with questions.

"You going in for five years?" I asked.

"Four to nine." The guy nodded toward the defense attorney,

kept talking. "Your man here says I'll do five if I don't get hit at the parole board."

"Still, five years is a long time. Why don't you just run?" I was thinking out loud—not giving advice, just wondering.

"Run? You shittin' me? They got my mom's house, I'm gonna run? She'll lose her house. Then, top of that, already paid my bondsman fifteen thousand dollars, so I'm deep into it."

Like I said, I'd heard all about bail bondsmen in my dad's prison stories, but this was the first time I had a full handle on how these guys worked. It sounded like a good gig. I did the math in my head—funny thing about me and my ADD . . . I was always great with numbers—and it seemed like a sweet deal. The bondsman got a 10 percent fee on the $150,000 bond, plus he had a kind of hedge against the guy's running because he had the mother's house as collateral.

Soon as the guy left the office, I turned my questions on our team's sponsor, started pumping *him* for information: "What, there's like one guy you recommend to your clients? The same bail bondsman, over and over?"

"Pretty much."

He gave me the bondsman's name, said he'd put me in touch. I was one of his best players, he wanted to keep me happy, so he told me he'd try to set up a meeting.

I walked out of there thinking that all you needed to be a bail bondsman was a big set of balls and a decent-enough gut to tell the difference between the guys likely to jump from the ones likely to stay put. Sure enough, my sponsor did set up a meeting, only I had to borrow my father's car to get there. I think I borrowed one of his ties, too—and $60, because I figured I'd have to spring for lunch. My father didn't see why I was getting together with this guy, didn't see how I could turn bail bonds into any kind of career. Plus maybe he'd seen enough at Rikers to question why I would want to point my life in this direction. But mainly he was always dissing me, putting me down, saying, "Ira, you're going nowhere. Be a gym teacher. That's what you know best, sports."

*Be a gym teacher*. It was like a mantra with my father—his answer to everything when it came to my career. He might have been right. Maybe I should have been a gym teacher, but I'd seen the kind of life my old man had as a teacher. It was respectable work, rewarding work, came with a decent, steady paycheck, but that was where it ended. I wanted something else, something more. Didn't know what the hell it was, or where to go looking for it, but I knew to keep looking.

I took the bail bondsman to lunch at a pasta place in the Bronx—not exactly high-end, but it was what I could afford. The guy went a little crazy on the menu: chicken française, salad, broccoli, fried calamari. When the waiter finally got around to me, I just asked for a salad. I didn't think I'd have enough money to cover the bill, didn't even think I could afford the extra three bucks to get some grilled chicken thrown on top.

Guy talked around and around without saying much of anything. Clearly, he didn't want some young punk like me stepping on his game, so he kind of stiff-armed me. He took the meeting because the defense attorney was a big source of business for him, so he had to at least go through the motions of helping me, but he wasn't about to clue me in.

The bill came to $54.86—I'll never forget it. Hardly left me enough for a tip, but I left what I had and counted the lunch as a loss. Still, I wasn't frustrated enough to give up on the bond business, not just yet. I went back to our softball sponsor and begged for another referral, and it was the same thing all over again. Borrowed another bunch of money from my father, another tie, and got another runaround in return. This time I got the message, and I figured I'd move on, throw another something against the wall.

Six months later, I was at a weekend tournament in Belmar, New Jersey, just off the Garden State Parkway. We played two or three games on a Saturday afternoon, then went out and got hammered that night, expecting to be at our best for another two or three games on Sunday. That's kind of how these things went—a lot of ball, a lot of drinking, a lot of craziness—only this one time I almost didn't make it out of bed on Sunday. We'd gotten back to the hotel at about five o'clock in the morning; figured I'd catch a couple hours' sleep before our eight o'clock game, so I stopped by the front desk and arranged for a wake-up call at seven. Keep in mind, it's not like we were staying in any kind of high-end hotel; there was no alarm clock in the room I could have used for backup, so I was relying on the guy at the front desk. Big mistake. Seven o'clock rolled around and I was still dead asleep. Seven thirty, my teammates started to worry. Quarter to eight, they came banging on my door and dragged me out of the room, and on our way through the lobby I gave it to the guy behind the desk pretty good.

It was the same guy from the overnight shift, and I lit into him. "What the hell kind of shithole you running, can't even handle a simple wake-up call?" You know, the kind of thing you yell at eight in the morning when you're still hammered from the night before. The kind of shit that doesn't deserve an answer.

The guy just forgot, was all, but I kept at him, and as I was ranting and raving, a sweet red car pulled up just outside the lobby. A Bentley, I think.

Guy behind the desk saw me looking at the car, so he pointed to it. "You want to make a complaint, talk to him."

An old man stepped from the car to the lobby like he owned the place, because he did. He was frail, moving kind of slow, but it didn't seem to matter. He had it going on.

Guy behind the desk went to say something, like he wanted to stir up trouble, throw me to the wolves, but I stepped in and started to make a joke over how upset I'd been. My teammates, they knew me as a clown, a cutup, so I tried to make everyone laugh. Turned to the old man and said, "What kind of mileage that thing get?" Meaning the Bentley.

The two of us, we got to talking. I had a game to get to, but something about this old man struck a chord, so we made some small talk as my teammates threw our gear into their cars.

I said, "Sir, if you don't mind me asking, where'd you make your money? I'm thinking real estate, right?"

"Afraid not, son. Bail bonds."

I thought, Bail bonds! I heard those words as some kind of sign—telling me I shouldn't have been so quick to give up on this notion a couple months back. Telling me maybe I was meant to pursue this line of work. I said, "You're kidding me, right?" Like this old man had any reason to bullshit me.

"Not at all. We're based here in Jersey, but we do business in the city, all five boroughs. All over."

I dropped the name of the first guy I took to lunch, the guy who'd ordered half the Pasta Lover's menu. "You know him?"

The old man nodded.

I dropped the name of the second guy I took to lunch. "You know him?"

The old man nodded.

I pointed to our team manager, who was settling the bill at the front desk. "Our sponsor over there, he's a big criminal defense lawyer in New York. You know him, too?"

The bail bondsman nodded again. "It's a small world, son. Walk around in it long enough, you know everybody."

The old man was the go-to guy for bonds in the whole metropolitan area. He said he was the bank—said it just like that, "the bank." Like I was supposed to know what the hell he was talking about. Wasn't blowing smoke or sticking out his chest, just telling me how it was. Guy had no reason to boast, that much I could tell. With our gear all loaded, my teammates were honking the horn, telling me it was time to pull out. I shook the old man's hand, asked him if I could call on him, took a card from the desk clerk, wrote down the guy's name and phone number. The whole time I'm thinking, Must be some kind of sign—me, oversleeping; me, running into this guy; me, giving up on bail bonds just a couple months earlier. The universe was trying to tell me something, I thought.

Turned out this Bentley guy, Phil Konvitz, pretty much ran the bail bond industry, if you could even call it an industry. He was based in Newark, but his business reached all the way across the river into New York, all five boroughs. At eighty-four, he knew everyone. Everyone knew him. It's like he was the mayor of bail bonds.

I thought maybe he could open a door for me, so I called him that Monday. I was twenty-nine years old, living with my parents, wasting away . . . why wouldn't I call? What the hell did I have to lose?

First couple times, I couldn't get through. Left two or three messages. Next day, I left two or three more. Finally, I got him on the line, reintroduced myself. Poor guy had no idea who I was, that's why he wasn't returning my calls. So I told him, "I'm the guy you met over the weekend, the softball player."

A light seemed to go on, on other end of the phone. He remembered.

We fell into talking. I pressed him about the business, about how to get started. He told me a bunch of stuff I'd already heard, but his tone was a lot more welcoming than what I got from the bondsmen I'd taken to lunch a couple months back. It's like what he was laying out for me was doable, within reach, and with those other guys it was like me banging my head against the wall. It was the difference between possible and impossible.

He ended the call telling me I should reach back out to the first guy I'd taken to lunch: "Tell him Mr. Phil said to call."

So I did. Left another couple messages. Every day, two or three messages. Finally, after about a week, I got a call back. These bail bond folks, what I was getting, they didn't exactly jump to return a phone call—unless they knew what they'd find on the other end of the line.

"We have a mutual friend," I said.

"Oh, yeah. Who's that?" Like the guy couldn't give a shit.

"Mr. Phil."

Dead silence. Then, after a long-ass pause, the guy said, "How do you know Mr. Phil?"

So I told him the story—and for some reason, the story made it seem like I didn't know Mr. Phil all that well. Like I'd just run into him in the lobby of a hotel in Jersey, like maybe it was nothing for this guy to worry about, me reaching back out, dropping such a big name.

I started getting the same runaround I'd gotten over lunch. I had to take the test, he told me again. I had to jump through this or that hoop. Wasn't a whole lot of money to be made, the whole thing was more trouble than it was worth, and on and on.

Next, I tried the second guy I'd taken to lunch, and it was the same deal. Told him we had a mutual friend, dropped Mr. Phil's name, waited for the dead silence, and soon we were going through the same motions as before. After a while, this second guy said, "Look, Ira. No, bullshit, there's no money in this business. You'd be better off getting a hot dog truck."

"What are you talking about, a hot dog truck?"

"Kid, I'm telling you, those hot dog trucks make a fortune."

"Thanks, but I'm not getting a fucking hot dog truck."

Right after I hung up the phone with the second guy, my mom came into the kitchen and asked why I looked so upset. I told her the quick version of the story, how I'd run into this guy who was like the mayor of bail bonds, how he told me I could call, how he'd sent me running into the same brick walls as before. She was curious, saw that I'd left a business card on the counter, reached for it. She turned it over and tried to read the name I'd written on the back—but my handwriting was so lousy she could hardly make it out.

She studied the card for a bit, scrunched up her face like she was thinking something through, then handed the card back to me. "You sure you got that name right, Ira?" she asked.

"Yeah, I'm sure."

She spelled it out, reading off the card. "Phil Konviz. K-o-n-v-i-z. Kind of an odd name, don't you think? You sure it's not Konvitz? K-o-n-v-i-t-z? You know, with a *t*."

I flipped. Don't know why, exactly, but I went off. Started

screaming at my mother like she'd just lit into me. I had no idea she had any kind of hunch about this guy, that she thought she knew him. I just thought she was busting my chops, same way my father was always busting my chops, telling me all I was good for was to be a gym teacher. "What the fuck does it matter how the guy spells his name?"

Wasn't like me to curse and vent like that in front of my mother, wasn't how I was raised, but I guess I was sitting on about a case worth of bottled-up frustration.

"Calm down, Ira. I'm just wondering about the name, that's all."

"Fuck the name. You don't believe me it's Phil Konviz? Konviz, K-o-n-v-i-z. That's the guy's name, okay?"

To prove my point, I got back on the phone to call Mr. Phil's office. By now, I'd gotten used to the way his secretary answered the phone. ("Hello, Bonding"—like, old-school, with a raspy smoker's voice.)

She recognized my voice, seemed to want to put me off—the way of the bond business, I was learning. "He's in a meeting."

It was bullshit, I think I knew even then. "Tell me something. How does Mr. Phil spell his last name?"

She spelled it for me, and I wrote it down on a little scratch pad by the phone. Sure enough, there was that *t* in there, the one my mother had been looking for. Just to be clear, I said it out loud like a question, emphasizing the second syllable: "Kon-*vitz*?"

"Konvitz," the secretary said.

"K-o-n-v-i-t-z? With a *T*?"

"That's right."

Surprised the hell out of me that my mother was right about such a small thing. "Are you sure?"

The secretary said, "Son, I've worked for the man for thirty-eight years. I'm pretty sure."

I thanked the woman for her time and her patience, told her it wasn't necessary to leave a message. Then I hung up and turned to my mother. "How did you know I'd spelled his name wrong?"

"Let me show you something." She took me into the living room and reached for this little wedding album she kept on the coffee table, started flipping the heavy pages until she found what she was looking for. She pointed to one of the pictures. "Is that your Mr. Phil?"

I couldn't believe it. It'd been over thirty years, but there he was, right there in one of the formal table pictures. It made no sense to me at first, but then I put two and two together, came up with something close enough to four. "I don't get it. We're related, he's a friend of the family, what?"

Apparently, my mother's grandmother had come over from Russia with Mr. Phil, way back when. They were cousins—and like a lot of immigrant families that came to this country in bunches, they stuck together for a while. Until they didn't. Our families had fallen out of touch after my mother and grandmother went to see Mr. Phil at his office in Newark. They went to see him because my grandfather was in jail. My mother dropped this little bombshell on me that afternoon, right after she showed me her wedding album. I'd had no idea. Apparently, my grandfather had been a kind of slumlord, back before the phrase was even coined, got into business with a bad guy, got into some trouble with the city, got himself locked up for a couple days at Rikers Island. Like I said, this was all news to me, all this time later, but my mother walked me through what happened. Told me how they had no money to bail out my grandfather, how they remembered they had this cousin in the bail bond business, how they took the train out to Jersey to see if he could help them. In those days, "Uncle" Phil wasn't doing bonds in New York, but he couldn't turn away family. He gave my mother and grandmother the $5,000 they needed, in cash, to get my grandfather out of jail—only the way my mother remembered it, they never paid him back.

"He was at our wedding," she said, "but we've been too embarrassed to keep up contact. Your father, he didn't like it that we owed him so much money."

I didn't know what to make of the connection. It was unlikely as hell, but it sure as anything seemed like a sign from the universe, telling me this was a path I was meant to follow.

I mean, incredible coincidences don't just up and bite you in the ass for no good reason, do they?

First thing I did was reach right back out to my long-lost uncle. Or cousin. Or whatever. My mother told me to tell him I was Rosie Cohen's great-grandson—Bubbe, we all called her. That would be the door-opener, she said. But before I could get Phil Konvitz to open any doors, I had to get him back on the phone, and this was no easy thing, getting past his raspy-voiced secretary. This was back in the days before Caller ID, but this woman must have had a sixth sense whenever it was me on the line—and here I was, calling back just a half hour or so after I'd pumped her on the spelling of her boss's name.

"I just told you, young man, Mr. Phil is in a meeting." She didn't sound too happy to hear from me.

"Please. Please, I know I've been kind of a pain, I know I keep calling, but I just learned the most amazing thing. Please, just hear me out."

Happily, amazingly, unbelievably . . . she did. And, for some reason, she bought into my story. She told me to call back after five o'clock that afternoon and she'd put me through. At precisely 5:01 p.m., not wanting to appear too, too anxious, I called for the third time that day, and this time the secretary actually sounded happy to hear from me: "I knew this would be you."

Right as he got on the line, I said, "Uncle Phil!"—a little too loud, a little too enthusiastic, a little too much. Soon as I said it, I wished I could pull it back and unsay it.

"Who the hell is this?" he asked, not surprisingly.

"It's me, Ira. Ira Judelson." Like he might have been expecting my call.

He didn't know what to say to this, so he called for the secretary. Her name was Dolores, I now learned, because Mr. Phil just about screamed her name—right into the mouthpiece. Dolores hurried into his office, I guessed, and started explaining the family connection, same time I was scrambling to do some explaining of my own from the phone in my parents' kitchen. I've got no idea how either of us managed to make ourselves understood, but the old man picked up on a word or a name that let him think I wasn't full of shit.

He said, "Bubbe Cohen? How do you know Bubbe?"

I started to tell him, but before I could get too far along in my story, he put me on hold. He didn't tell me he was putting me on hold. He didn't say anything, I just heard a click and a whole lot of silence. I thought maybe he'd hung up on me, but it didn't make sense that he'd hung up on me because he'd seemed to be plugged in to my story. Anyway, the connection didn't cut out so I stayed on the line. After a couple minutes, I heard another voice—some guy named Jerry Watson, said he worked with Mr. Phil, was one of the vice presidents of his company. Jerry Watson spoke with a thick Texas drawl, started asking me a whole bunch of questions: my Social Security number, my mother's maiden name, my place of birth . . . He didn't say as much, but I got the feeling he thought I was some kind of con artist, trying to shake down this elderly millionaire, and he was some kind of gatekeeper, on the payroll to keep Mr. Phil from this kind of nuisance.

Finally, when he ran out of questions, Jerry Watson said he'd call me back and abruptly hung up the phone.

A couple hours later, the phone rang. Same guy. "Be in our offices Monday morning, nine o'clock."

Monday morning rolled around, and you can bet I was right outside the office, with plenty of time to spare. "Uncle" Phil worked in the heart of downtown Newark—One Newark Center, right next to Seton Hall Law School. His company was called International Fidelity Insurance, and as I rode the elevator to the twentieth floor, I saw that they occupied four entire floors in this big-ass building. They did construction bonds, corporate bonds . . . all kinds of bonds, but the twentieth floor was dedicated to bail bonds, and it was huge.

The way a bond works, just so you know, is straightforward. It's like an IOU. The holder of the bond is the lender—or *creditor*. The issuer of the bond is the borrower—or *debtor*. Doesn't matter if it's a bail bond or any other type of bond, it's the same basic transaction. One party lends money to the other, or the promise of money on behalf of the other, in exchange for interest or a piece of property or some other form of collateral. The back-end terms are negotiable, and they change each time out. These days, I don't get involved in any type of bonds beyond bail bonds, but when I first met him, Uncle Phil was into all kinds of shit. He wrote a lot of insurance bonds and traded in all kinds of municipal and treasury bonds—but bail bonds were the "juice" of his business.

It's how he made his name, where he liked to spend his time—and what he liked about it, mostly, was that it connected him with all kinds of people.

I'd read up on him before heading out to his office. Wanted to make sure I was up to speed, so I actually went to the library and looked him up. Learned he'd written the bond for Amy Fisher, the "Long Island Lolita," who'd been charged with the attempted murder of Mary Jo Buttafuoco, the wife of her boyfriend. For a while, it was all over the television. Bail was set at $2 million—a record number at the time—and this was Phil Konvitz's biggest claim to fame. The guy had been at it for over fifty years, had a choke hold on all the bail business in the New York area. He'd done thousands of bails, yet this was what he was known for—posting the bond for a teenage girl in the middle of a tabloid scandal.

He ran a pretty big operation, my uncle Phil. Soon as the elevator doors opened, it felt like I was stepping into this teaming, pulsing workplace. It was like a factory—or, better, like the trading floor of the New York Stock Exchange. Of course, I'd never been to the floor of the New York Stock Exchange, so what the hell did I know? I only knew that the place was filled with energy and excitement—nothing at all like me sleeping late and going about my half-assed business out of my parents' kitchen.

This was big-time stuff, and I wanted in.

The boss came out to meet me. He had his hand out in greeting, but I blew right past the handshake and collected the old man in a hug. "Uncle Phil!" I said—again, a little too loud for the occasion, but I was way past caring. The guy was family. More than that, the guy was opportunity. I don't think I'd ever been so excited to see someone.

When I let him go, Uncle Phil stepped back and held out his palms, like he was surrendering. "Well, you found me."

"Yep, I found you," I said with a huge-ass grin on my face.

Uncle Phil put his arm around me and began to walk me back toward his office. He said, "Son, tell me what you want to do."

I couldn't think how to answer. Oh, I knew what I wanted, but I couldn't think how to put it into words, so I just came out with it. "I want to be a bail bondsman."

"Okay," he said. "Done. You're a bail bondsman."

Just like that.

# 3

# No Bail Too Big or Too Small

Okay, so maybe I didn't become a bail bondsman just like that, but that's the short version. The longer version has my wife, Blake, in it. Matter of fact, she's all over it. We'd just started seeing each other a couple weeks before I started seeing Uncle Phil, so she was with me the whole way—encouraging me, inspiring me . . . kicking me in the ass.

To this day, I've got no idea what Blake saw in me. I didn't have all that much going for me other than a good time when we met. I was still living with my parents and bouncing between odd jobs. I'd just turned thirty, and Blake wasn't even twenty-one. She was still in college. I thought she was the most beautiful girl I'd ever seen—just a knockout. But she was also smart, and funny, and she had a great big heart—which also knocked me out, not to be corny or anything. On paper, our relationship made no sense. When I met her, Blake was running all over the place, doing telemarketing, going to school. She was a go-getter, and right away I started to think she was light-years ahead of me in the getting-your-shit-together department. Her parents thought the same thing—well . . . her mom, at least. I guess they liked me well enough, her parents, but they didn't think I'd amount to much. For years afterward they kept telling Blake to keep her options open—to where her mother was once hospitalized and even asked a young doctor for his phone number for her daughter (when I was sitting in the same room!). But I didn't let it bother me. I understood. They only wanted what was best for their daughter—and back then, I wasn't even close.

Logistically, we didn't make sense, either. Blake lived on Long Island, Uncle Phil was out in Jersey, and I lived up in Westchester, which meant I was mostly on the road, ferrying back and forth. It's amazing I found any time to study for my licensing test, which was administered by the New York State Insurance Department, which is now part of the Department of Financial Services. Uncle Phil had his guys hook me up with a bunch of old tests so I could prepare. There was nobody to coach me, no class or program to help me study, so I had to rely on these old tests. One section was multiple-choice questions, and another was essay questions—a lot of stuff that felt all the way out of reach to me at the time but now feels like a part of my own skin:

**Q: Which individual is the least desirable candidate for bail—a white-collar criminal, a rapist, or a shoplifter?**

**A:** A shoplifter, because of the three he probably has the most transient lifestyle, which makes him the most likely flight risk.

Q: **Does the bondsman have the right to** *revocate* **a bail bond?** *Meaning, can he revoke a bond on his own, without the consent of the court?*

A: Yes, if the bondsman is in receipt of new information that leads him to believe a client is a flight risk or a danger to the community—or the client has not answered to his civil contract. *Meaning, he's failed to show up for a court date or an appointment with the bondsman—and meaning, too, that I had to open up my dictionary of legal terms to figure out what the hell* revocate *meant.*

Best I could tell, the focus seemed to be more about the nuts and bolts of the criminal justice system than about the day-to-day of being a bondsman. There was a lot to cover. It brought me right back to how I felt in school, left me feeling all squirmy and rebellious and out of my element. My first instinct was to look for a way to bail, or maybe find my way around taking the test, and if it weren't for Blake, I don't think I would have made it. I looked at the material, and it could have been nuclear physics, but Blake coached me through it.

She'd call every night and say, "Did you study today?" Making me take my medicine.

I'd say, "Yeah, some." Or maybe I'd lie and say I put in a couple hours, just to make it sound good, but whatever I said Blake could hear in my voice if I was telling the truth. The bullshit detector on her? Man, it was something. It's like she knew me her entire life instead of just a couple months.

On weekends, I'd drive down to her place on Long Island and we'd study. All I wanted to do was fool around, but Blake was tough. It's not that she didn't want to fool around, too, but she wouldn't let it happen until I took a few practice tests. And I couldn't just *take* the damn tests—I had to pass them, too. She made up a set of flash cards to help me study, and I'm almost ashamed to admit it, but I'd never even *heard* of flash cards, fuck actually using them.

She said, "What, you've never used flash cards before? Do you even know how to study?"

All I could do was shrug—and follow Blake's lead.

This went on for a couple weeks. Meanwhile, I kept driving out to Uncle Phil's office in Newark, just to poke around. I wanted to soak in the atmosphere, learn what I could. Also, I wanted him to see my face and see that this opportunity was important to me. Turned out it was important to him, too. Each time I walked in the door, he'd say, "You ready to take the test? You ready to take the test?"

Like it was him getting this great opportunity instead of me.

The year I took it, the test was given at the library in White Plains. A bunch of different tests were being offered that day, and maybe ten or twelve people signed up in total, so it's not like this was a hive of activity. It was a big deal to me, but it wasn't any kind of big deal in the room, and I walked out thinking it could have gone either way. Some stuff I didn't know, and I couldn't even guess at some stuff, but I had many questions down cold, thanks to Blake and her flash cards and whatever scraps of information I'd been able to pick up at Uncle Phil's office.

Two weeks later, I got a letter in the mail telling me I'd passed, but I didn't get to enjoy the victory too much since I still had to deal with a major roadblock: I had a criminal history. I didn't know this would be an issue. Like an idiot, I didn't think they'd run my fingerprints—never even occurred to me. See, I'd gotten into a few bar fights in my day, had some assaults on my record, some trespassing charges. The personal identification charge meant I'd got caught trying to pass a fake ID. Nothing to be proud of—but if you're thirty years old and spent some time working in a bar, you're bound to have some kind of history.

Uncle Phil called me with the news. He sounded pissed. Wasn't like him to sound pissed. "Why didn't you tell me you had a record?"

"I'm sorry, Uncle Phil. They're just bullshit charges."

"Come into the office. We need to talk about this. You can't work for the state if you have a record."

The whole way out to Newark, I was sweating, frantic, nervous as hell. Whatever shot I'd had at the bond business, however close I might have come, these troubles in my rearview mirror left me thinking I'd blown it. When I got to his office, Uncle Phil couldn't even look at me. I could tell he was pissed. I could tell I'd let him down. Typically, when I'd go out to visit with him, he'd tell me stories. His mood would brighten and he'd get to talking.

The guy loved to talk. Sometimes, he talked about running around in Cuba with Meyer Lansky, Lepke Buchalter, Lucky Luciano . . . he knew them all back in the day. All those Murder, Inc., guys—those were Uncle Phil's first clients. He'd built his business on the back of organized crime. Things were different back then, he always said. There were no such things as surety hearings—which have pretty much become standard operating procedure, when you go before the court and prove the money for the bond isn't coming from any ill-gotten gains. Also, old-school judges would never set cash bail, which they do nowadays in cases when a defendant is considered a flight risk but the law dictates that a defendant must be admitted into bail. The "mechanics" of the business were a whole lot looser, too. A lot of times, Phil would go straight to the precinct and do the bails right there, instead of in front of a judge. Always, there'd be a "tax"—Uncle Phil's term for the juice he had to pay to his wiseguy friends. He'd never call it what it was—a shakedown. No, in his mind, it was a tax, the cost of doing business, the price he had to pay to move into a new market, a new city. So he paid, without complaint. In return, his "friends" never made a move without him. Ended up, he ran Asbury Park, he ran Newark. He ran New York City. For fifty years, he had the whole metropolitan region wired—taking him up to that $2 million bail for Amy Fisher, which put him on the map all over again.

Best I could tell there'd been some wild times along the way, although Uncle Phil's stories were sometimes tough to follow. He was starting to struggle with Parkinson's, which I didn't know at the time, but it was becoming more evident by the day that something wasn't right.

I fumbled to explain myself. "I'm so, so sorry. I had no idea they'd run a check. I really screwed up, huh?"

Uncle Phil wasn't making it easy for me—and I guess I had no right to expect him to make it easy for me. I knew he'd helped me along, and now I'd let him down, and on top of that I'd let Blake down, and the ride back across the bridge to my parents' house in Westchester was agonizing. I still didn't have my own car, so I was driving my dad's gray Nissan Sentra and crying like a baby. This was back before everyone had an E-ZPass, so I remember waiting in a long line to pay the bridge toll, and every couple seconds the car behind me would start honking like crazy for me to move because I couldn't get my mind focused. I kept thinking how I'd screwed up, how here on in my life would be one long stretch of hopeless crap. How Blake would finally listen to her parents and find someone else. How I'd be stuck living with my parents forever.

I just felt so hopeless, man. Hopeless and helpless and all the way up against it.

Somehow, I made it home that night without smacking up my dad's car, and first thing I did was reach for the phone and call Blake. Told her how I'd messed up, how sorry I was, but she was great about it. Said to give it some time, said not to beat myself up over something that happened years ago. Nothing in her voice led me to think she was through with me or fed up. Just disappointed, she said. For *me*. For *now*. She couldn't have been more supportive. It was way more than I deserved.

I didn't call Uncle Phil the next day. I was too ashamed, too chickenshit to hear whatever might have been waiting for me on the other end of the line. So what did I do? Mostly, I sat in my room and fidgeted. Watched a little television. Went to the gym. Stared at the damn ceiling.

Next morning, Uncle Phil called, his voice sounding like it did before he found out about my record. Like things were back to how they were. Either he'd forgotten, or things had worked themselves out. Either way, it didn't much matter. I heard in his voice that we were good, so that's how I played it.

"I'm so sorry, Uncle Phil. You stuck your neck out for me. You believed in me. I let you down."

"Don't worry about it, kid. We'll take care of it."

"What do you mean, we'll take care of it? Two days ago you said I was finished. Said I'd never get a license."

"That was two days ago. Today, it's a different story."

The different story was that Uncle Phil would make all these charges disappear—*poof!* There'd been six dispositions in all, and they would all go away—but first I'd have to run around to six different police stations to get copies of all the paperwork. Then, I'd send the files out to Uncle Phil's office, and he'd take care of the rest. To this day, I've got no idea what he did, how he managed to bury my record. My guess is, he probably hired a lobbyist in Albany to push me through the licensing board.

For a couple weeks, I didn't hear anything. Finally, I got a call from the Department of Insurance, some guy telling me I had to come in for an interview. One more ring of fire to jump through. Soon as I sat down for my appointment, it was clear this guy was out to bust my balls. He had all my paperwork spread out on the desk in front of him. "What's all of this?"

Like he didn't already know.

"Those are dispositions, sir," I patiently explained to him. "To be completely honest with you, I had some trouble with authority when I was younger, but that was a long time ago." I'd decided to be honest, apologetic—only it didn't look like such a good strategy right out of the gate.

"A long time ago, huh?" the guy said, coming at me. "Six arrests, these kinds of charges, tells me you've got a temper."

"Respectfully, sir, that used to be the case. But like I said, that was a long time ago."

"Temper like that, doesn't always go away." Then, like he was trying to bait me: "If I spit in your face right now, what are you gonna do about it?"

"Nothing, sir." I wasn't biting.

"Oh, you're a big man now. You've got family in the business.

You think you're above the law?" Laying on the sarcasm, the attitude.

I don't know if this guy was good at his job or just a huge asshole or maybe both. He kept trying to wind me up, but I wouldn't let him. After a while, he gave up: "You'll hear from us in a couple days."

One week later, my license arrived in the mail. My golden ticket. It was a simple certificate—no bells and whistles, no ceremony, no little hats with tassels. But I couldn't have been happier. It was the greatest feeling in the world to set my sights on something and grab at it. Wasn't used to that kind of result away from a ball field. That little piece of paper opened all kinds of doors for me, eventually—and the thing of it is, I knew just by holding it in my hands that this was how things would go, here on out.

Wherever I'd been, wherever I was going . . . I'd arrived.

At first, Uncle Phil wanted to set me up with the bondsman from Westchester who'd met me for lunch and couldn't have been less interested in helping me. All of a sudden, the guy wanted me to work for him—probably to get in good with Uncle Phil. But he was only offering $400 a week, which wasn't a whole lot of money. I was thirty years old. I wanted to move out on my own, maybe start in on a life with Blake . . . $400 a week just wouldn't cut it. So we went back and forth on this for a while, and I went from thinking this license was the greatest thing ever to thinking it was just a piece of paper, after all. I didn't have the chops or the credit to go out on my own. I needed work.

After another stretch of back and forth, Uncle Phil called me into his office. He handed me a contract.

"What's this?" I said, like an idiot.

"It's a contract," he said, like he thought I was an idiot.

He'd worked it out with another office he ran, this one in Manhattan. Said he'd pay me $1,000 a week. It was all laid out in the contract. All I had to do was show up. What the contract didn't say, what nobody seemed to want to tell me, was what the hell I was supposed to do when I got there.

The two guys who ran the place worked for my uncle, except they liked to hide that they worked for my uncle. It was their shop, but he was the money, so I don't think they were too happy with me being installed right outside their office. They took it like I was there to spy on them. I didn't think that was the case—but, again, what the hell did I know? More likely, Uncle Phil must have felt he had the juice to insist they take me on, at a halfway decent salary, so he made that happen.

In addition to the two owners, there were two front-desk girls, an office manager, a secretary, and three other bondsmen. Nobody talked to me. The whole first day on the job, nobody said a fucking word. Nobody even looked at me. It was the strangest thing. I kept staring at my watch, desperate for five o'clock—wondering, nine to five, how I was supposed to fill the time.

End of the day, Uncle Phil called to see how things went. "How they treating you down there?"

"Fine, I guess."

"Fine, you guess?"

"Well, nobody will talk to me," I said, giving it up. "Nobody will even look at me. They think I'm there to be your eyes and ears."

"Hang in there, kid."

I thought, What choice do I have?

Next day, it was the same thing all over again, only this time

Yvette, one of the office girls, stopped by my desk after lunch and said, "No one's gonna talk to you, you know."

"Kinda figured that."

"They think you were sent by your uncle to find out what's going on."

"Kinda figured that, too. So what *is* going on?"

"You don't want to know."

No, I didn't. I just wanted to do my job.

(Actually, strike that—I also wanted to *know* how to do my job.)

Yvette took care of me after that. Told me how to write up a bond. Told me what to do in court. Told me how to put in for my expenses. Whatever wasn't covered on Blake's flash cards, whatever I couldn't figure out on my own, Yvette laid it out for me. She was terrific—for whatever reason, she took a liking to me, and fifteen years later she's still helping me out, still the heart and soul of my Manhattan office.

She called in another bondsman, some kid younger than me, said she wanted him to look out for me in court. The deal was he'd tell me where to go, how to raise my hand, how to present my paperwork. Kid didn't much want to be my babysitter, but Yvette made it seem like it wasn't up to him, like the request was coming from the top, so he did like she asked. For a couple weeks, I followed this kid around, and every night I'd get home and Uncle Phil would check in for a report.

"How they treating you down there?" he always asked.

Gradually, I learned my way around the courthouse. Technically, I was still under this kid bondsman's wing, still following his lead, but I was off on my own a lot of the time. Wish I could remember the very first bond I wrote, but in those days it was mostly nickel-and-dime stuff. Tough to tell one case from the other—all pretty much routine. Uncle Phil would ask me how many bonds I wrote each day, and I'd count them off for him. Some days, it was three or four. Some days, five or six. He didn't care about the number, I don't think. He just wanted to know if I was making out okay.

Six or seven weeks in, our office was robbed—at least, that's how it went down. The cops came. The owners kept a lot of cash in a safe, and they were crazy-sick with worry. Said they'd lost tens of thousands, maybe more. Cops asked a lot of questions, but the case never went anywhere. I didn't know enough to consider that there might be something *off* about the claim. I didn't understand the business, how to trick the system, but I knew enough to know I didn't like these guys Uncle Phil had in charge. At first, I didn't like them because they didn't like me, but by now there was something else. There was something dirty about them. Couldn't put my finger on it, but it didn't make sense, their being so concerned about a nephew of the big boss getting started in the business. Yvette hinting that something was going on I didn't want to know about. From my first day in the office, it's like they were all hiding something.

I didn't say anything to Uncle Phil about how shady the place seemed when I first started, mostly because I couldn't think what to say, but a couple weeks after the burglary I started bringing it up in our nightly phone conversations. I'd say things like "Something smells wrong in here." Or "How well do you know these guys?" Nothing specific, nothing he could act on, but I just wanted to get him thinking along these lines, let him know *I* was thinking along these lines. I don't know, maybe I was hoping he'd put two and two together on his own, work it out that these guys were cheating him. The thing is, those first weeks on the job, I didn't know enough to understand what they were doing, but after a while even I could see what was going on.

They were writing a bunch of fake bonds that they were putting through alongside their legitimate business. It was a pretty crude operation. They'd take actual bonds down to Kinko's and make a bunch of color copies. All denominations—$5,000 and under; $10,000 and under; $25,000, $50,000, $100,000 . . . all the way up to $500,000 in a couple cases. They'd take these copies and submit them to the court, and since the copies had actual power numbers on them—meaning, tracking and ID numbers that corresponded to legitimate cases—they were put through, and for the dummy transactions these guys would collect their usual fee from Uncle Phil's insurance company, so they had their hands in his pockets in a bunch of ways.

The whole office was dirty, just about—except for Yvette. She knew what was going on, but she also knew not to say anything, didn't think it was any of her business.

Once I was sure of the situation, I put it to Uncle Phil: "These people are stealing from you."

I'll never forget the harsh tone he used, answering me: "Don't be a rat." Like he didn't want to know—worse, like *I* was the one stepping out of line. Like I'd broken some kind of code. So eventually I stopped bringing it up in our nightly calls, and Uncle Phil didn't press me on it.

I'd been on the job three or four months. I'd been green for the first month or so, suspicious for the next month or so, and quiet ever since. These assholes were stealing, I was sure of it, but I didn't want to be a rat. Figured Uncle Phil knew what he was doing—only he wasn't doing anything, not that I could see.

Then out of nowhere, I got a call after lunch at the office in New York from Dolores, Uncle Phil's secretary. "Mr. Phil wants to see you."

She'd called him *Mr.* Phil, I noticed—what she called him to everyone else, what everyone else called him. To me, she always referred to him as "your uncle Phil," so I thought maybe this was some kind of tell. Left me thinking maybe I'd messed up in some way and I was being called out to Newark for a dressing down—like being dragged to the woodshed.

I pressed Dolores for some information. "Is anything wrong? Did I do anything wrong?"

"I'm just the secretary, Ira." Her go-to line whenever she wanted to stiff-arm a question.

I thought, This can't be good. I'm fucked.

Before leaving the office, I called Blake. "I fucked up again. Uncle Phil wants to see me."

"What happened?" she asked, concerned. Not angry.

"That's the thing. I've got no idea."

"So how do you know you fucked up? You're reading into it. Maybe he just wants to see you."

"Middle of the day? Me, here in Manhattan. Him, sending for me. Dolores was like 'Get here as soon as you can.' What else could it be?"

Blake tried to calm me down, but when I get a thing in my head, it finds a way to stay there until I give it a reason to leave—and telling me I was reading into something was no reason, so when I hung up with Blake, I was no closer to being rational.

The whole way out to Newark, I couldn't think what I'd done wrong, what was waiting for me across the river, how I could face Blake or her parents after the shitstorm came down—and probably the only thing I was sure of was that there *would* be a shitstorm.

I was shaking in the elevator up to the twentieth floor. It was the longest fucking elevator ride of my life, and I remember thinking it wasn't long enough. I didn't want those doors to open, to face whatever was waiting for me.

But those doors opened eventually, so I stepped out to meet my fate. Dolores took me back to Uncle Phil's office, where he was waiting with my two "bosses" from the Manhattan office, and a couple key guys from the Newark office. I thought, Great, a regular lynch mob. It's not enough Uncle Phil's called me in to chew me out and fire my ass, but he's about to do it in front of the whole damn company.

Uncle Phil stepped out to meet me, put his arm around me. Like always, he was dressed sharp, styling—expensive suit, polished shoes . . . all the way down to the smart-looking pocket watch he used to carry. Let me tell you, he cut an impressive figure. The other bondsmen, they dressed off-the-rack, but not my uncle. He took time with his appearance, kept telling me how important it was to make a powerful first impression. And he *walked the walk*, this guy. Even now, the hammer about to come down on my brief career as a bondsman, I had to admire my uncle. He stood apart—almost like he was playing the game on a whole other level.

He gestured for us to take a walk. We went down the hall away from the office where the lynch mob was waiting. Walked past my cousin's office—Norman, Phil's son. We stopped, and Uncle Phil stepped back and looked at me, like what he was about to say was hard for him. "I'm not gonna be here much longer, Ira."

I thought, What? Where's the part about me fucking up?

Where's the part where he fires my ass and makes an example of me? What the hell is he talking about?

What he was talking about was his declining health, his mind slipping away from him, his career winding down. I couldn't think what to say, so I said nothing.

"Don't know what it is, Ira, but you got it. You got street and you got smarts, both."

I thought, Okay, this is a surprising turn. Maybe it's not as bad as I thought. Maybe he didn't call me in to chew me out. I still couldn't think what to say, but figured I should make some kind of noise, just to let Uncle Phil know I was listening, so I said, "Thanks."

Whatever was coming, I told myself I was ready for it—only I wasn't *exactly* ready for what came next.

Uncle Phil pointed to Norman's office. "Always take care of Normie."

I couldn't think why this was on me, taking care of Norman. But I didn't want to miss a chance to let my uncle know he could count on me, so I said, "You don't have to worry about Normie." It was something to say, but underneath it there was a lot more. I didn't know where to start, so I just went for it. "What the hell's going on, Uncle Phil? Why'd you ask me out here, middle of the day? Why are all those guys in your office?"

He turned back toward his office and waved his hand dismissively, like he had no use for all those people. "They're out, you're in."

"What do you mean, 'They're out'? Where are they going?"

"What do you care where they're going? Out. Away. Gone. You, you're in."

For the first time in my life, I was tongue-tied. Seriously, hope-

61

lessly tongue-tied, like in the cartoons I used to watch as a kid, all done up in knots. If my career depended on it, I couldn't have said a fucking word—only the thing of it is, my career *did* depend on it, and I still couldn't say shit.

It was like I was "made"—like a scene out of *The Godfather*, only this was no movie. This was my life, my career, all about to spill from this one moment, from the kindness of one old man who turned out to be family, who had for some reason taken a liking to me, and who had for some other reason taken me on and now seemed to want to set me up as the head of his New York operation.

Here I'd been thinking I was about to be sent packing, and the whole time my uncle had something else in mind. He laid it out for me. The two guys from Manhattan, they could no longer write for him—meaning, Uncle Phil would no longer insure their bonds. They still had the lease on the Manhattan office, so they could try to hang on and hang in, but once word got around, they were as good as done. Business would dry up. Uncle Phil had the lease on the Queens office, so that would be my base of operations starting out while I looked for a place in Manhattan. I could keep on whoever I wanted, let go whoever I wanted, hire whoever I wanted.

It was too much to take in, and I said so. "Uncle Phil, I've got to be honest. I don't know anything about the business."

Really, I knew *nothing*—at least, nothing to leave me feeling I could make good. I caught a reflection of me and Uncle Phil in the glass of a picture frame, and what I got back was unsettling. Him, looking all dapper and polished and confident as hell. Me, looking disheveled in a discount suit, my hair a mess, my nerves all shot to hell. Me, twice the size of him—and him, twice the man as me.

"What, you don't want it?"

"No, I want it," I said, trying to shut out that reflection. Trying to carry myself in my mind like Uncle Phil.

"Good."

We shook hands.

He took me into his office and we sat down at his desk, working over figures on a scratch pad. "The girl. You'll probably want to keep her on."

"What girl?" Then I realized what girl. "Yvette?"

"Yes. She's good." He wrote down a number—her salary and benefits. "That kid in the Queens office, you'll probably want to keep him on, too."

I didn't know if I wanted to keep the kid in the Queens office, but I just nodded and looked at the number Uncle Phil wrote down for him.

Then he put down numbers for rent and other expenses and showed me the scratch pad. He pointed to the total. "That's what you'll need to run the office, first year"—about $100,000, more money than I could get my head around. More money than I'd ever seen, but that was about to change. Uncle Phil told me to take $100,000 from petty cash and put it in the bank. "You'll pay me back when you can."

Next day, Ira Judelson Bail Bonds opened for business.


One of the first headline-type bonds I wrote out on my own was for a young guy from Queens named John Taylor. It was a tiny, nothing bail—$3,500. I wrote it without even thinking about it, same way I handled a lot of my business when I was just starting out. The kid had been caught with an unloaded weapon. Didn't have a record. Didn't have any reason to run. It was less than a year after my uncle had set me up in business, and I was grabbing whatever bonds I could, whatever came my way, and this one felt like a no-brainer. Didn't have any reason *not* to write it. All I thought about was the $350 fee I'd collect, and how far it would go toward covering my rent, my nut. I was making payments on the $100,000 loan from Uncle Phil, but Ira Judelson Bail Bonds was barely making it. I couldn't afford to turn down a fee, so long as it made at least a little bit of sense.

The bail bond business works different in every state. In other states, bondsmen can make 10 or 15 percent on the bails they write, but New York has a 6-8-10 structure—meaning, the higher the bail the lower the percentage. Up to about $50,000, we collect a 10 percent fee, then it goes down to 8 percent at $50,000 as it approaches $100,000. North of that, we charge 6 percent, on top of any number of fees and surcharges associated with the bail. The big bails are where most of our good business is, and that's where we can make a name for ourselves, so that's where we want to be, but we can't ignore the small stuff. These four-figure bails are like our bread and butter, our piecework, especially when we're new to the game.

So I wrote this bond without thinking about it, but the way things turned out, I should probably have thought about it. I kicked myself over that decision for years to come. Why? Because while this kid Taylor was out on bail, he and a buddy walked into a Wendy's fast-food restaurant in Queens and killed five employees. It was May 24, 2000. The murders made news all over the country, especially in New York, where the story was on the front page. The murders were shocking, sickening, grisly as hell. The victims had been taken into a basement freezer. Their heads were wrapped in plastic bags. They were shot at point-blank range. Police responding to the call said it was one of the most brutal crime scenes they'd ever seen.

John Taylor had been a manager at that Wendy's location, so he knew his way around, knew exactly where they kept the keys, the safe, whatever. But this also meant the police were able to pick him up within a day or so of the murders. He and his accomplice, Craig Godineaux, had shot two other employees, who survived. One of them made the 911 call and was able to identify Taylor, who'd made off with about $2,000 from the restaurant safe. Taylor was arrested at his sister's house on Long Island and ultimately convicted on twenty counts of murder and attempted murder. When Supreme Court justice Steven Fisher signed a death warrant for Taylor, he became the first person to be sentenced to death in Queens since New York reinstated the death penalty in February 1995. His sentence was later commuted to life imprisonment.

The story was huge, out of control—and it was all over the news that I'd written this guy's bond. I set it up in my head that I was responsible for the deaths of all these innocent people. It shook me up. I couldn't sleep, couldn't eat. For the first time, I started thinking about what I now did for a living in terms of its impact on society. Before John Taylor, it was just about pushing paper, managing risk, making enough money to provide a nice life for me and Blake. All I cared about was whether it made sense to write this or that bond. Was it a good risk? Was there sufficient collateral? Was I covered in the unlikely event that my guy jumped? It never occurred to me to consider the client's guilt or innocence. The nature of the crime, the charges against . . . none of this shit mattered to me, and I thought back to all the conversations I'd had with Uncle Phil about the business and realized it didn't much matter to him. If I thought about this type of stuff at all, I probably put it on the judge. If a judge didn't think someone was fit to walk the streets, he wouldn't set bail. But now one of my clients had gone out and killed five people—shot them in the head, in cold blood. Shot two other people, too. And I put him back on the street.

How do you live with *that*?

Uncle Phil tried to talk to me about it, but I couldn't listen. He kept saying, "You had no way to know." This was true, but it didn't help. It didn't help because it left me thinking of all the other bonds I had out on the street, all the other bad guys, and how there was no way to know about each of those cases, either.

"Look at the people I'm dealing with, Uncle Phil," I said. "Sick motherfuckers, a lot of them."

"A lot of them, yeah. But a lot of them are innocent. Don't ever forget that. A lot of them shouldn't spend another night in jail, away from their families."

I didn't give a plain shit about the innocent people awaiting their day in court. I didn't care about the *justice* part of our criminal justice system. I only cared about John Taylor and the people who'd worked with him at that Wendy's. I tore out an article about the murders from the *Daily News* and carried it with me. Looked at the thing so often I memorized the names of Taylor's victims: Jean Auguste, Ramon Nazario, Anita Smith, Jeremy Mele, Ali Ibadat. Ja Quione Johnson, just eighteen years old, in critical condition with a bullet in his brain. And Patricio Castro, the guy who'd survived and called it in.

Blake couldn't talk me down from whatever I was thinking, feeling. She tried—better believe it, she tried. Told me it wasn't my job to be judge and jury. Told me not to beat myself up, blame myself. Told me all the things I needed to hear, but I couldn't hear them at the time. Not yet. Not for a good long while.

"There'll be other John Taylors," she said.

"Thanks, that helps," I said, meaning it was no help at all.

"Let me finish, Ira. There'll be other John Taylors, but if you don't post bond for them, someone else will. If you can't deal with this, first time out, it'll kill you eventually."

She was smart, my Blake. Don't know that I was ready for such an in-your-face take on what I'd chosen to do for a living, but there it was. In my face—like it or not. Help them or don't—but know that somebody will.

We'd gotten married six months before, me and Blake. We were still newlyweds, and she was serving up these giant helpings of advice and support like she'd been married to me her whole life.

And she was right—I was just doing my job. It was a good bail. It was good on paper, good in the room. John Taylor snapped, was all. Yeah, he snapped while he was out on my authority, snapped while he was my responsibility, but that he snapped . . . well, that wasn't on me. Not really.

For a long time, I couldn't see it this way, but I came around, and I had Blake to thank for it.

# 4

# Early Days

First couple years after Uncle Phil helped me hang out my shingle, I could do fifty, fifty-five bonds in a week, maybe sixty. I was hungry, hustling, trying to make a name for myself. These days, I process about thirty, thirty-five a week. Multiply that out over fifty-two weeks, it gets close to two thousand bails each year—still a big number, and those numbers keep adding up. Some of these bails stay open for two or three years, depending on how long each case takes to snake its way through the courts, so at any one time I might have five or six thousand open liabilities—meaning, clients on the street whose freedom has been secured by one of my bonds.

By *me*.

To put what I do in perspective, there are probably a hundred licensed bondsmen in New York State—maybe forty to fifty in New York City alone. The number is constantly changing because a lot of fly-by-nighters are in this business, and a lot of folks are licensed to operate but don't have an active operation. Of that number, I'd say about a dozen are owner-operators of their own business, like myself, with offices in the greater metropolitan area, including Nassau and Westchester Counties. At the high end, among the established bondsmen, it's an everybody-knows-everybody deal. At the low end, with so many people coming and going, I've never even heard of half of them.

Sometimes, cases can stretch on even longer than a couple years. One of my clients might go into a drug program and the judge keeps the bail open until he finishes, or maybe a case takes years to get to trial. Or maybe there's new evidence or the investigation takes some new turn and the case grinds to a crawl.

It'd be tough to put a dollar number on all those open liabilities, but I'd guess a conservative estimate would be that it hovers around $60–$70 million. I don't care if you're a legal loan shark, like me, or if you're just a plain old loan shark—that's a lot of money to have out on the street, but that's how it shakes out. Whatever that number is, I'm exposed on a good portion of it. Technically, I'm exposed on *all* of it, together with my insurance company, because if the defendant jumps, we're on the hook for the full amount. That's why we spend so much time putting together the bail package—the collection of assets friends and family of the defendant bring to me to secure the bond.

If the collateral's right, we're mostly covered. Trouble is, the collateral isn't always right. Generally speaking, in a declining real estate market like we just had, the longer a bail stays open, the more I'm screwed. Why? Let's say I write a $500,000 bail against a house with a market value of $750,000, with about $200,000 left on the mortgage. That's cutting it close, even at the time I put the package together, but if the real estate market tanks, I'm undercollateralized. If that $750,000 house is suddenly worth, say, $500,000, I'm left holding a $500,000 bond with a house that's now only worth $300,000 to me, after subtracting the $200,000 owed on the mortgage. So you learn early on to look at other factors in determining if a case is "good" bail. You assess the risk. If the client is solid, if he's not running, if he's got a support system in place, like family, putting up a piece of property or a business . . . you take all these factors into consideration and give yourself a kind of cushion. You do your homework, you develop a feel for human nature, for the work, you learn to minimize your risk. You'll take a chance on a kid because you'll see you're not really taking a chance at all. Maybe the numbers don't add up, but your gut is telling you this kid's not going anywhere. Or maybe the collateral is solid, or they're putting up cash, but you don't trust the client, or his lawyer, or whatever; it feels like more trouble than it's worth.

It's a trial-and-error deal—and in the beginning there was a whole lot of error.

First piece of bad business I ever wrote was for a punk I'll call Ramon—a big-time Dominican drug dealer from Washington Heights. The cops picked him up after he'd been shot, so things were already bad for Ramon when I was called in on this. Bail was set for a half million, which would have made it the biggest bail of my young career, so I was like one of those wolves you used to see in those old Warner Bros. cartoons, licking my chops at such a big payday. I don't think I had had more than a half dozen six-figure bails, so the thought of *these* six figures sent me spinning. Eventually, the bail was reduced to $250,000, which was still the biggest bail I'd ever written—meant about $15,000 to me, with my 6 percent fee.

All that money in one place was enough to cloud my judgment. I didn't do my due diligence. The kid had a pretty girlfriend, might have left me thinking, Hey, why would he run, with a girlfriend who looked like *that*? Plus, since Ramon's initial bail had been reduced, I knew he was cooperating, which meant he'd be looking at a much lighter sentence—maybe even no jail time at all if his information was good. And his family came forward right away with a pizzeria they wanted to put up as collateral, so I put it all together in my head and decided to do the bail.

I made a bunch of rookie mistakes on this one. The biggest was that I didn't look deep enough at the pizza business. Like an idiot, I didn't look at the lease the right way and misread that the family owned the building where the pizzeria was located. I didn't look at this kid the right way, either. He'd been shot, so I should probably have figured he was in this thing pretty deep.

I thought I had it covered, but I thought wrong.

I'd been doing bonds for just a year or so, and I used to run everything by Uncle Phil—well, maybe not everything, but certainly everything big, and this bail was pretty damn big, so I laid it all out for him. Told Uncle Phil about the pizzeria, what it was supposedly worth, only I didn't show him any of the paperwork. He would instantly have caught what I had missed. Not only did the family not own the building where the pizzeria was located, but they didn't even own the ovens or the tables . . . just the dough, the sauce, the pepperoni. Everything else was leased, so basically the business was worth shit, only I didn't know this at the time. All I knew was that the business was making money, and that Ramon's lawyer told me his client was a good kid. The girlfriend, too, had good things to say about him—but what the hell did I expect? Any girlfriend is bound to tell you her boyfriend is a stand-up guy, so she wasn't the most reliable judge of character, but I felt this girl had an integrity, a genuineness, that left me thinking she wouldn't waste her time on a guy who'd jump.

Uncle Phil didn't trust me yet to call my own shots, but he trusted me enough to let me follow my gut. Two hundred and fifty grand was a big number for me, but it was a number my uncle could absorb. I understood that he had to ride shotgun with me for a while, and I appreciated the confidence. His big thing was to be on the constant lookout for a bad bail. He used to say, "Kid, you can write nine good bails in a row, but it's that tenth one that'll kill you. Never get excited by the number."

Uncle Phil used to tell me a bogus piece of property doesn't always bite you in the ass, as long as the client doesn't go anywhere, and that you can misjudge someone's character and still be okay, long as you have a good bail package to back you up.

It's when both sides of that equation go bad that you're well and truly screwed, and here I was well and truly screwed. For a while, Ramon did what he was supposed to do, went through the motions same as every other client. He showed up in court, checked in with me, did everything by the book. Then, about six months in, I got a forfeiture notice, telling me he'd missed a court date. I flipped out, went back, and checked Ramon's card—the file I keep in-house, tracking the comings and goings of each and every client—saw he'd missed a meeting with me the previous month. The way it works, so many open bails, it's impossible to track each and every one proactively. The system has alerts that tell you when something's wrong, when a case has gone off the rails, but at that point you're already fucked—and here I was, already fucked.

First thing I did was call Ramon's lawyer. I lit into him pretty good: "Where the fuck is your client?"

Next call was to Uncle Phil because I couldn't let this thing unravel any more than it already had without cluing him in. He needed to know. I'd catch a bunch of shit for it, but he needed to know. He didn't go off on me. Just listened to what I had to say, said to think of it as a hard lesson, said to keep him posted.

Then I reached out to a couple of the bounties I used at the time, to get them on the case. Bounty hunters are a last resort in my business. You bring them in when you can't locate a "jumper" on your own—and they pretty much work like the name suggests. You put a bounty on the head of whoever's at large—typically, a percentage of the bond—and the bounty only gets paid if he brings the defendant in.

(Out of that, the bounty has to cover his own expenses, on spec, although if he gets my client back into custody, I'll usually find a way to reimburse him.)

In practice, you sometimes "hire" two or three bounties to work the same case, and they kind of duke it out. It's like an episode of that show *The Amazing Race*, only they're chasing bad guys instead of prizes. It's like any other business. There are good bounties and not-so-good bounties. There are guys with a background in the military, in police work, in procedurals, and then some loose cannons whose only related experience might be working as a bouncer.

You get what you pay for, and since you don't pay for anything going in, sometimes you don't get anything in return.

I'd already had a few jumpers, but nothing of this magnitude.

In the beginning, I used to tag along, chase the bad guys down myself—until I got myself shot at by some punk-ass kid during a search of a run-down house in some shit neighborhood. Luckily, the kid missed, but I tore out of that run-down house like it was on fire, nearly got hit by a cab as I raced into the street, and when I told Blake about these near misses later, she gave me all kinds of shit: "I did not sign up for this, Ira!"

When Ramon jumped, I was working with two bounties named Eddie and Billy—rough-and-tumble types. Uncle Phil had hooked me up with them. I filled them in on Ramon's story, gave them all his information, waited to see what they'd turn up. After a while, I called in another bounty, Tom Evangelista, and he's the guy who eventually found Ramon.

Like I said, in the bounty-hunter business, whoever brings the guy in gets the "bounty," so Eddie and Billy were out of luck. They'd had a running start, but Tom beat them to it, and that's just how it goes when it's every man for himself. These days, I don't like to call in more than one guy at a time because I don't like to screw anyone out of a fee, but if it's a big bail and I'm exposed on it, I'll cast a pretty wide net. With Ramon, these guys found out he was cooperating all over town. Wasn't just this one case, either. The kid was working with the Manhattan DA's office, making his court dates, checking in with me on schedule, but then the DEA grabbed him on some other charge, started squeezing him for information, too. That's when he ran. That's when word got around that the kid was a snitch—not a good thing to have on your résumé when you travel in these circles. The Latin Kings and a couple other gangs Ramon was involved with put out a KOS on him—a "kill on the spot" order.

The kid freaked—understandably, I'll admit, but at the time I didn't give a shit about *understandably*. I just cared about the bail, and the shit I'd catch from Uncle Phil for overreaching on this one. And the court, they just cared about the body—specifically, about getting that body back into court.

Tom Evangelista finally found Ramon hiding in a kind of hamper in the apartment in Yonkers belonging to the girlfriend's mother. It was like something out of a bad movie, the way this kid knew these bounties were after him, the way he was ducking into all these nooks and crannies, desperately trying to save his ass.

Me, I was trying to save my ass, too, only we didn't grab Ramon in time to avoid some steep penalties. In New York, you have a full year from the date of the forfeiture notice to catch the defendant and remand him into custody, but the bail laws in New York are some of the toughest, strictest in the country. Underneath this one-year deadline, there's also a 120-day "grace period," where if you bring him back in that time, it's up to the judge to determine a fine, which can be any number up to and including the full amount of the bail. These days, a lot of the judges I work with will waive the bail because all they care about is the body—in other words, they take a no-harm/no-foul attitude. They'll cut you some slack because you've been able to turn things around. But back then they didn't care about the body so much—it was more about the principle, the letter of the law. A defendant jumps, he's on the run for more than 120 days, the bondsman is on the hook—even if we catch the guy before the full year is out.

In this case, it was almost nine months since Ramon had jumped, so it's not like we were cutting it close. We'd shot all the way past that 120-day sell-by date, which meant I had to file something called a remission notice and hope to reach a settlement with the state. There was an argument to be made on both sides, could have gone either way. They could have charged me the full amount of the bail or waived the fee entirely, or anything in between, so we settled smack in the middle. Ended up costing me a buck and a quarter, this kid jumping on me, and once I realized I wouldn't see a penny out of that pizza joint, I had to go back to Uncle Phil and ask him to cover me. (By this point, the pizzeria had actually been sold.) There's no way I could get close to that number on my own, so he gave me a bridge loan, which he just added to a bunch of $10,000, $20,000, $30,000 loans I already had open with him, putting me deeper and deeper in the red.

I could have challenged the ruling on this, but nobody thought I'd win. The state could basically do what it wanted. They could have charged me the full amount, so I had no choice but to take this deal. Wasn't a good deal, but I told myself it could have been worse.

Now, the thing with Uncle Phil's business, it wasn't a one-man-band operation. He had partners, people he had to answer to. These guys were looking at my ledger, at all these bad bails I'd been writing. In fairness to my rookie, green self, it's not like I was writing a *ton* of bad bails, but the dozen or so in the first year were enough to give Phil's partners pause, especially since they were starting to run into serious money. And now that they were looking at this $125,000 fine on Ramon, they started to tell my uncle maybe he'd made a mistake, setting me up in business. One of his partners said, "Phil, this kid's bad news. I think we should cut him."

(*Cut him* as in "let me go"—hey, it's not like Uncle Phil and his partners were about to come at me with a knife, even though I did have more than a half million dollars in forfeitures.)

But Phil kept supporting me, backing me. Kept telling everyone I was family. It's a line they'd all gotten used to hearing—but in relation to his son Norman, not to me. Phil was always backing Norman, and always kind of griping about it, so I started to feel like I'd let my uncle down—in general and in this specific case. He'd been all excited when we first caught Ramon, before it came clear the state was gonna jack us up for half the bond, but even then he covered me. He was angry, frustrated I'd done such a piss-poor job putting together this kid's package, reading his situation, but he kept reminding me I was young, I was new at this, I had a lot to learn.

Up until this business with Ramon, Phil and his partners had given me some rope, but now they tightened things up. Now they wouldn't let me write a bond above a certain number—for a while, that number was $100,000. It didn't matter that I was family . . . this was business. Can't say I blamed them. Guess I needed a couple checks and balances to keep me from screwing up. Yet, even with all these constraints, I managed to grow my game. I got better at reading people. I was more careful with the property. I was a sponge, soaking up everything I could about the business, about the court system, about what goes on in and around the prisons. And I was pounding the pavement. It helped that I came along at a time when a lot of the old-guard bondsmen in town were dying off or retiring.

There were opportunities for an aggressive guy like me, especially after I figured out how to get in with the right people. In the bail business this meant people on both sides of the fence—from defense lawyers to *known associates*. Working through Uncle

Phil, I got known to a number of big-time defense attorneys, guys like Gerry Shargel and Murray Richman, Ben Brafman and Ron Fischetti, Jerry Lefcourt and Jimmy DiPietro, Joseph Corozzo and Frank Rothman, Pete Frankel and Joe Tacopina, Arthur Aidala and Lawrence Digiansante—not exactly household names beyond Canal Street, but if you were in a jam and had the money, these guys would go to war for you.

First year or so I was in the business, a lot of these guys started sending me work—probably because of their relationships with Uncle Phil. It was more of a what-the-hell, let's-see-what-the-kid-can-do referral approach than any sort of bet on me that I was the best guy for the job—but I didn't care. It was work, which meant there'd be money coming in. I'd skulk around the courtroom, looking for any opportunity, any excuse to get in a word with one of these top attorneys, because they could make or break you in this business.

Most times, the attorney sets up his clients with a bondsman, so I wanted to be the first guy on their Rolodexes—and, yes, this was back when people still used Rolodexes. I'd corner Ben Brafman, for example, and start pumping him with questions for information. "Mr. Brafman, it's an honor to meet you, sir," I'd say. "I know you use Irv Newman or Bob Baretta, but I'd love to do your work."

I made it a point to learn which lawyers used which bondsmen, so I tried to match my pitch to the situation, made sure the names I was tossing around were the right names.

"I'll be there twenty-four/seven for you, sir," I'd say. "I'm just starting out. All I need is a chance."

One lawyer took me aside and told me I looked like a bum—not in so many words, but his message was clear. Most of these established defense attorneys dressed to go to court like it was an Armani fashion show, while I just threw on whatever I had in the closet, and this one lawyer looked me up and down and said, "Kid, you've got the gift of gab, but you've got to do something about your clothes."

Bail bondsmen like myself, we were hustling, street types. Typically, we didn't go in for fancy clothes, but the better lawyers were all about making an impression, I started to notice. They needed to impress the judge, the jury, the press—and in some ways they needed to look a little sharper, a little more imposing, than the lawyers on the other side of the case. Some kid working as an assistant district attorney didn't have the kind of money to dress to the nines like these guys, and I could see a little bit of intimidation going on between these two camps. The "bad" guys were being represented by these slick, polished clotheshorses, while the City of New York (the "good" guys) was being represented by a bunch of weary public servants in ill-fitting suits.

For whatever reason, the message took. I wanted to stand out, to play on a different playing field than the other bail bondsmen in town—and one good way to do that, I realized, was to dress better. A look in the mirror told me a makeover would give me an edge. I was wearing a $99 suit from Today's Man, which was where I bought all my suits. They looked cheap and didn't fit me right—even I could see that. It had never occurred to me that this was something to pay attention to. To me, a suit was a suit, didn't matter if it was custom-fitted or off-the-rack, but I had to listen to these guys.

I didn't have a lot of money, but I scraped together what I could and bought a bunch of nice suits, some shirts, a couple decent ties. Enough to get me through a week in court, and then I could mix things up and cycle through my wardrobe all over again

Don't know if it was the new clothes that did the trick, but more and more business started to come my way.

Once, early on, Gerry Shargel gave me a chance on a $5,000 bond. It doesn't sound like much, and it wasn't, but Gerry represented John Gotti Jr., Puff Daddy, Sammy "the Bull" Gravano . . . even Enron. Heavy hitters across the board. So I jumped at it. I went out at one in the morning to do this $5,000 bail for him, and from that day on the calls kept coming from his office. It's like something switched, like I'd passed some sort of test.

Soon after that, Ben Brafman called—said he was reaching out at Gerry's recommendation—and for him I bailed out a rabbi client who needed to get out before *Shabbes* started on a Friday night, and I remember we were scrambling, trying to get all that paperwork in before sundown . . . and after *that* I was in good with Ben.

Those two guys, Ben Brafman and Gerry Shargel, got my name out there. From them I was officially in the book—and from them I learned a whole lot more than just dressing the part. From them I learned how to read my clients, how to separate the good cases from the ones that merely made headlines or promised a little bit of a payday. From them I learned how to carry myself—how to put it out there that I had my clients' backs. The better defense attorneys, like Brafman and Shargel, were all about doing the right thing. Most of them, that's why they started working that side of the law in the first place; some of them might have forgotten that, but the better ones kept it front and center. It wasn't just about the case with them. It wasn't just about winning or losing in court. It was about treating their clients with respect and going out of their way to see that they got a fair shake.

• • •

Wasn't so easy to walk that ethical road—whether or not I looked the part.

Soon, I started running with a whole different crowd. More and more, I'd find myself working with alleged wiseguys, well-known gangbangers, white-collar criminals . . . my clients ran the gamut, had their fingers into everything. Sometimes, we'd become friendly. Not go-away-on-vacation-together friendly—more like guess-I-should-invite-this-guy-to-my-kid's-christening friendly. Sometimes, they'd want to set me up, show their gratitude, take good care of me. I knew enough from my lawyer pals not to accept any favors, but I wasn't above making the best of my new situation. Long as I could pay my own way, I told myself, I'd go along for the ride, and in this spirit I started going to Rao's, the famous Italian joint in East Harlem that was probably the toughest restaurant in New York to get a reservation.

Rao's was a see-and-be-seen-type place when I was just starting out, same way it is today. Mobsters, rappers, athletes, Wall Streeters, celebrities of every size and stripe . . . they all wanted a table at Rao's, and I was just plugged-in enough to know what it meant, getting invited to this place. It was like a notch in my belt, being asked in among this crowd—took it as a sign I had arrived.

First time I had the opportunity to go, Blake and I were just engaged, but my invitation wasn't exactly a "plus-one," so I left her at home. I kept calling her all night long, each time someone famous walked through the door—someone I knew she'd give a shit about.

"Blake," I whispered into the phone, trying to be inconspicuous, cool. "Mariah Carey just came in, with Gloria Estefan."

"Blake, Jim Carrey's here, with Danny DeVito."

"Blake, you'll never believe it. John F. Kennedy Jr. is here."

Got to admit, I was a little starstruck myself, but mostly I knew Blake would have gotten a real charge out of it, so I kept calling her. When I noticed Tommy Mottola, the famous music industry executive who was married to Mariah Carey, I had to call Blake and report my latest sighting.

"Oh my God," she screamed. "Ira, you've got to get him my tape."

I guess I should mention here that Blake was a singer—and not just a *singer*, but a really, really talented singer. She was tremendously talented, if you want my unbiased opinion, and it wasn't just me who was knocked out by her voice. For a time, she had a contract with Elektra Records, but they could never find the right vehicle for her, the right sound, and she was kind of treading water in her musical career.

More than anything, Blake wanted to hop into a cab and come up to Harlem, but I didn't like the idea of her traveling alone, that part of the city, that time of night. More than that, I didn't have the juice to bring her along to this private dinner. So I put her off, told her I'd see what I could do.

I've since been to Rao's dozens and dozens of times, but this was an epic night. Jim Carrey and Danny DeVito were in New York filming the Andy Kaufman movie *Man on the Moon*, so there was a whole table of cast and crew, celebrating DeVito's birthday. John F. Kennedy Jr. and his wife, Carolyn Bessette, were there, with a group of people from his magazine, *George*. At another table were Tommy Mottola, Mariah Carey, Gloria Estefan, Céline Dion . . . All these beautiful, talented, successful people bunched together in this one small room.

Great food, great wine, great conversation—just great on top of great.

The more we all drank, the more all these different groups of people started to mix and match. Jim Carrey started doing scenes from *Dumb and Dumber*, and everyone was laughing and singing and having a wild time.

Finally, Tommy Mottola got up to go to the bathroom, so I thought I'd follow him. I was drunk, not thinking too clearly, but I wanted to do right by Blake. Back of my head, I was thinking like a *macher*—like I could put these two people together and make things happen. Didn't occur to me that it wasn't cool to approach a guy like Tommy Mottola in the bathroom of Rao's and touch him up for a favor, but even if it had, I would probably have done it anyway—that's how much I wanted to make this one thing happen for my girl, help her realize her dreams.

I hung back for a beat, then barreled through the men's room door a couple steps behind Tommy Mottola. No, this wasn't cool, but I was determined to play it cool—as cool as possible, anyway. I nodded as we made eye contact through the mirror. "Hey, Mr. Mottola. How's it going?"

It was just something to say.

He nodded back. "Call me Tommy. You guys look like you're having a good time." Meaning me and the others at our table, where the *Man on the Moon* crowd had kind of gravitated. The whole place was loud and raucous that night, but our group was kind of leading the charge.

"You can say that again." The conversation was going nowhere. We went about our business, but I didn't want to let this opportunity pass. "Mr. Mottola, sir, I hate to bother you on this, but my fiancée is a singer. She's great. I'd love it if you could listen to her tape."

As soon as I said it, I felt like a dumb-ass—and Tommy Mottola put me right in my place: "Could I put my penis back in my pants first?"

It was a great line, only I didn't have it in me to laugh. Not at the time. And Tommy Mottola was great about it. I'd put him on the spot, but he was classy. "Tell you what, kid. Send me the tape. Write that we met here at Rao's, at Danny DeVito's birthday party. I'll be sure to listen to it."

Like I said, classy.

But Blake never followed up, never sent her tape. Always thought she was a little embarrassed, the way this opening came about. Doesn't exactly make the best how-I-got-this-gig story, right?

End of the day, though, the music business just wasn't in the cards—for Blake, for *us*. Our lives were headed in a whole other direction.

# 5

# Babies and Bonds

About a year after Ramon jumped on me, Blake was pregnant with our first child, and I had a foot in what was going on at home and another foot in one of the biggest corruption scandals in New York history. I was still deep into hustling mode, trying to get my name out there, grabbing every piece of work that came my way, but I was also caught up in the expectant-father thing. I wanted to be present and available for Blake and the new baby *and* to be a good provider for them, so I was being tugged and pulled in all these different directions.

This exciting, crazy time led to the wildest night of my early career—and one of the most memorable nights of my life. Around eight o'clock that night Blake went into labor, and we rushed over to Einstein Hospital in the Bronx. While they were getting her ready, I ducked out into one of the hospital hallways to check my phone. In those days, 2001, they made a big deal about shutting off your phone in the hospital, so a nurse flagged me down, told me I could be messing with patients' pacemakers and all that. So of course I shut the thing off.

Our daughter Ava was born at about nine thirty the following morning, and Blake and I were crazy with happiness. Oh, man . . . Ava was such a precious little thing. Just perfect. And Blake was doing great. I couldn't have been more excited, and as soon as the nurses got Ava all cleaned up and settled in Blake's arms, I raced out to the waiting room to tell my parents, my in-laws. I was bursting with our good news. They'd been there all night, and I kept running back and forth to give them updates, so I was excited to tell them they were grandparents—and soon as I did, there was a lot of hugging, a lot of tears. It was such a great moment, I only wished Blake (and, now, Ava) could have been a part of it.

Yet even in the middle of such an emotional high, my mind flashed back on that low-moment scene on my parents' doorstep, when my high school girlfriend stopped by with her kids on Halloween. Don't know why I was thinking in just this way, but somehow I made this connection, and I realized for the first time I felt like I was really and truly on my way, like I was making something out of my life. I'd thought I'd felt these things before—when I met Blake, when we got married, when things started to happen for me in the bond business—but not until I held this sweet, tiny baby in my arms, or until I celebrated with our parents, did it all kick in, all together, in just this way.

Then, as I made my way back to Blake and the baby, I reached for my cell phone and turned it back on—force of habit, I guess. I don't know why I was thinking in just *this* way, but that tug and pull between work and family must have been superstrong. I honestly don't think it occurred to me to check in with work, but I was so used to being plugged in, to having the phone at my side, I must have done it without thinking. Blake was always on me about this, even before the baby—said I should shut the thing off at night, said that whatever it was could wait until morning. She was right, but I was so determined to be successful, I was a little frantic I might miss a piece of business. I'm still the same way. I've always got my phone with me. Typically, when I flip it open first thing in the morning, there'll be two or three messages, so that's what I was expecting, and I was only paying half attention as the power kicked on and the screen started to fill.

You know how when you turn on your phone, the messages kind of load in, one by one? Well, that's what happened here, and I watched as the screen said I had one message, then two, then three . . . it just kept going. Ten messages, eleven, twelve . . . all the way up to twenty-six. Twenty-six messages!

I thought, What the fuck?

I had a brand-new baby waiting for me just down the hall. My beautiful wife was a brand-new mother, and she was waiting for me, too. But I stopped short of Blake's room to take care of business. The tug and pull was too strong. I just had to listen to some of these messages, see what was going on. That whole other plane I just mentioned? Me, feeling like my life was at last amounting to something? I must have gotten used to it pretty damn quick because I ducked into a small room where I didn't think I'd mess with anyone's pacemaker or any of the equipment and started listening.

First message: "Hey, Ira, it's Murray Richman. They just took down the Javits Center. I need you down here."

Second message: "Hey, Ira, it's Gerry Shargel. Call me as soon as you can."

There was message after message, from lawyer after lawyer, trying to track me down—eight or nine lawyers in all, and some of them had even left a couple messages, and on top of that I could see another dozen or so missed calls, folks who didn't even bother to leave a voice mail. Also, guys I'd grown up with, alleged wiseguys I'd known forever, had left messages like "My dad took a pinch and needs you right away. Please call."

First call I returned was to Don't Worry Murray—that's what everyone called Murray Richman. Behind his back, to his face . . . he carried the nickname like a badge. He was first in line, but he'd also been my biggest supporter. "Where you been, kid?" he asked.

I told him my wife and I just had a baby.

"Hey, how 'bout that! Mazel tov, kid. That's great." I could tell from his voice that he was truly happy for us—thrilled—but then he got right down to it. Told me there'd been a sweep of the Javits Center, an enterprise-corruption case, thirteen arrests—a big deal. Murray was representing four of the thirteen individuals charged in the case—most of them Italian, most of them with alleged ties to the mob—and he wanted me at the arraignment that afternoon.

"Murray, what about my kid? You know I'd do anything for you, but she was just born. Like, not even an hour ago." It's like I was asking him for advice and asking him for permission to let this one go, both.

"Right, right. Your daughter. Of course."

He didn't sound pissed or anything, but I could tell he wasn't expecting this. I'd always been there for him before, no matter what, so he naturally assumed I'd be there for him on this one. And I would have been. Any other day, any other time, I would have dropped whatever I was doing and had at it. But this wasn't any other day, any other time. This was just an hour or so after my daughter was born.

While he had me on the phone, Murray started talking to the people who were with him—in his office, in the courtroom . . . wherever the hell he was. I heard him say, "The bondsman, the young guy I use all the time, he just had a baby."

In the background, I could hear his Jewish lawyer colleagues shouting out cries of "Mazel tov!" and "Congratulations," and a bunch of other voices, probably belonging to his jammed-up, mobbed-up clients, saying, "That's fuckin' great!"

"Fuckin' awesome!"

"Well, what do you fuckin' know!"

I tried to listen in to all these separate, sideline conversations, but it was tough to hear what they were discussing. There was a lot of noise, a lot of activity. Finally, Murray got back on the phone. "You still there, kid?"

"Murray, what should I do? I don't want to let you down, you've been so good to me, but I can't leave my wife right now."

"No, you stay at the hospital. I'll call you back."

While I was waiting to hear back, I returned another couple calls. Gerry Shargel—same deal. A client jammed up on this Javits case, wanted me at the arraignment this afternoon.

Every call was about this case—which was all over the radio, all over the newspaper.

After a couple minutes, Murray called back. "Listen, kid, they're gonna stay in. They'll wait for you."

I wasn't sure I'd heard him right. "What? Who? Wait for me to do what?"

"My clients. On this Javits case. Said they'll stay in jail for the night, you'll take care of it tomorrow. Do what you have to do."

"Murray, they're doing this for me? I appreciate the business, like always, but there are other bondsmen. It makes no sense they should stay in jail any longer than they have to. There'll be other bails. I'll catch the next one."

He laughed, almost like he was dismissing my concerns for his clients. "Believe me, Ira, these guys, they wouldn't mind being away from their wives or their girlfriends for the night. Like a little vacation." He paused, let it sink in. "And as far as other bails, I don't think you'll see these kinds of numbers anytime soon."

I was young and green, but I'd been around long enough to know this wasn't *just* about ducking out on their wives for the night. Murray's clients didn't need to be in jail to stay away from home. No, they were stand-up guys, doing me some kind of solid—like a baby gift, was how it came off. They didn't know me from any other bondsman in town, but they knew Murray, and Murray put it out there that I was the guy to bail them out, that I'd just had a kid, that I could use the payday from such a big case.

"Thank you, Murray," I said. "You don't have to do this, you know."

"Don't mention it, kid."

I told Murray I could leave the hospital by six o'clock that night, get started on the paperwork, work through the night to make sure the bonds were ready to go first thing in the morning. For this part of the call, I was back in Blake's room as she was settling in with Ava, and she overheard me talking, flashed me this look that seemed to say, *This better be good, Ira.*

(That, or maybe it said, *What the fuck is wrong with you, Ira?*)

I didn't even wait for her to say anything when I hung up the phone, just went right into my song and dance. "Honey, I'm sorry, but it's a big case. Could be a lot of money for us."

Still, she didn't say anything, just turned her attention to the baby, to getting the room organized. Our parents were in and out, people were sending up flowers, balloons, whatever . . . so Blake was distracted, happy to show off little Ava, while I retreated to a corner of the room and continued working the phone. I had to call my insurance company and set up that whole end. I had to call Uncle Phil. I had to call my Manhattan office and get my office manager working on the families of these guys, work it out so they could come in and start putting together their packages.

Each time I got off the phone, I'd catch myself staring at my new baby daughter, wondering what the hell I was doing working the phone at a time like this, but then the phone would vibrate again and I'd have to take the call.

Blake didn't miss a thing. She saw what was going on, saw that I was torn up about it, so she didn't bust my chops any more than a little. She knew I couldn't let such a big piece of business slip away, and it had only gotten bigger after that call with Murray. Soon, the other lawyers heard about Murray's clients and convinced *their* clients to wait until the next day for me to bail them out. In all, I had eleven out of the thirteen cases, spread out among Murray and a couple other lawyers.

Together, Uncle Phil and I looked at the cases and figured these bails could be for as much as $100,000 each, maybe more. The insurance company still wasn't too happy with me over all those forfeitures, and Uncle Phil's partners weren't too thrilled, either, but my uncle told me he'd take care of it. He was excited about the baby, excited about all these bonds, excited to throw in on this. Already, the case was getting a lot of media attention, and when you're a bail bondsman this is a good thing. The bond business is like anything else—work leads to work, and high-profile work leads to high-profile work, so this was a giant opportunity for me. The timing was lousy, but as I left the hospital, I kept telling myself I'd make it work.

What the hell choice did I have?

Wasn't until I was in my office, getting the paperwork ready, that these seven other cases came my way, so now we had to add *that* paperwork to the mix. It takes a while to put a package together—a couple hours, if there's no tie-up—and here we had to prepare eleven of them. We were at it until midnight—me, checking in with Blake at the hospital every hour or so, partly to see that she was okay but mostly to see that I wasn't in her doghouse for ducking out on such an important moment in the life of our young family.

Next morning, I showed up in court in one of my new Hugo Boss suits and got ready to approach the judge, the Honorable Jeffrey Atlas, when the case was called. I knew Judge Atlas from a couple previous cases, and he always struck me as a by-the-book kind of guy—fair, but tough. Like a lot of judges, he expected you to act a certain way in his courtroom, to be prepared, to not waste his time.

The defendants in the case were walked into the courtroom in cuffs and instructed to approach the judge's bench. The prosecutor on the case was an ADA named Mike Scotto—we'd become friendly over the years, but this was one of the first cases we had together. First guy he called was an alleged member of an organized crime family, so Mike gave the charges and the circumstances. The courtroom wasn't set up for the arraignment of so many defendants all at once, so the court officers corralled them into the jury-box area, and when they were called, they were supposed to cross directly to the judge. I'd never met these guys, but my clients all knew who I was, and this first defendant didn't cross directly to the judge. Instead, he went out of his way to pass by where I was sitting and leaned over and whispered, "Pssst," to get my attention. "How ya doin', Ira? I'm Paulie." Then he pointed to a woman in one of the back rows. "That's my wife over there, waving. We just want to tell you congratulations on the birth of your daughter."

Next up was another made guy—same thing, crossed by where I was sitting. "How ya doin', Ira? I'm Frankie." Then he pointed to *his* wife, who was also waving, and told me how happy they were to hear my good news.

One by one, they passed by where I was sitting and took the time to say hello—time they didn't really have in Judge Atlas's court. All eleven of my clients came by to pay their respects on their way to the bench. Some of them told me they had their wives or girlfriends bring gifts for my wife and daughter—flowers, balloons, a little something from FAO Schwarz, some homemade wine or cheese. It was an unbelievable display—touching as hell, but also a little surreal. Why? Because these weren't just *any* clients. These were made guys, some of them. The rest were known associates, so for them to carve out this little ceremony in the middle of their arraignments was a real honor. It was a huge show of respect to me, and at the same time a huge show of disrespect to Judge Atlas, so as they kept up with this parade of congratulations, I started to worry it might piss the judge off. Most arraignments of this size take about an hour or so, and here this one was stretching to two hours and more . . . and I was so anxious about the impropriety of it I hardly noticed the numbers on the bails—$250,000, $150,000, $200,000, $100,000 . . .

The numbers were huge, and after the judge heard the prosecutor and set bail, I had to present the bonds to the clerk, and only then did I do the math and notice the total—approaching $1.5 million. I was blown away by the number, and as I went back to the judge to get him to sign off on each bond, I got a sick feeling in my stomach that something was a little *off* about this scene. It was like a circus, a little bit, the way these wiseguys were clapping me on the back and whispering in my ear and pointing out their wives. I worried Judge Atlas would find me in contempt because he was stone-faced the whole time. I couldn't get a read on his emotions, and then he called me up to his bench. He cupped his hand over the mouthpiece of his microphone and swung it to the side, and as he leaned over to talk to me privately, I thought he was about to chew me out for the behavior of my clients.

"What did you have?"

I didn't understand the question at first, and he seemed to read the confusion on my face because he followed up with another.

"The baby. A boy or a girl?" For the first time, I saw him smile.

"A girl, Your Honor. A beautiful baby girl."

"Congratulations, Mr. Judelson." Then he told me about his children, how he could still remember the days they were born, how I should cherish this moment . . . the usual stuff you hear when people find out you're a new father, only here it struck me as way, *way* unusual to be hearing this stuff from a judge presiding over an arraignment in a major corruption case.

"Thank you again, Your Honor. I'm a lucky guy."

Next, Judge Atlas leaned in a little closer, cupped the microphone a little tighter, and dropped his voice to a whisper. "I upped the bails a little bit to help you with your college fund." Then he winked.

It put me on the map, that one arraignment, the day after Ava was born. Wasn't just about the money, although it didn't suck that I stood to make about $90,000 in fees, which I had to share with my insurance company—still, a decent chunk for a single day's work. Wasn't just about the way Murray Richman set me up with all these guys, convinced them to stay an extra night in the joint just so I could be with my wife and kid. Wasn't just about the circus sideshow in the courtroom, me in the center ring. No, it was all these things, taken together, left me feeling like I was on top of the world.

All three of my kids would be born during a major organized crime case.

My son, Casey, came next, in 2004, just as the city was making a bunch of arrests in the bricklayers' union. Murray Richman represented three defendants in the case. The bails were similarly high, all set at about $250,000 each—$750,000 in all, with a fee to me of about $45,000. Of Murray's three clients, one was an alleged mob captain, one was the brother of the alleged captain, and the other was a well-known associate, but here the personal side of the story wasn't as dramatic as it was at Ava's birth. We weren't running to the hospital or frantically trying to put together a bail package in the middle of the night, but the drama found me soon enough. It came because the well-known associate decided he didn't have to pay me my fee. I'd already done his bail, and normally I take my fee straightaway, but because of who this guy was I figured I'd let it slide for a couple days. After about a week went by I called him up to collect.

"How ya doin'? It's Ira Judelson."

"Ira, good to hear from you. What's up?"

So I told him what was up, told him he owed me $15,000.

"Oh, that." Like he was dismissing it as no big deal, him being behind on such a big payment. "About that, I apologize. I should have it for you next week. They froze my house, all my assets, but I'll get it to you. I promise." For good measure, he added, "Don't worry, I'm not a flight risk."

I hadn't even thought to worry about this guy jumping—when you're in the family "business," you tend to stay put—but I owed the insurance company on this, and they were still keeping on top of me because of all those early forfeitures. I wanted to square things with them as soon as possible.

A week went by, I never heard from the well-known associate.

Another week went by, I never heard from the well-known associate.

Halfway through the third week, I put in another call. "How ya doin'? It's Ira Judelson."

I got back nothing. Not even a grunt in response. Then: "What the fuck do *you* want?"

I thought that was a strange thing for this guy to say, given our situation, thought maybe he had me mixed up with someone else, so I started in again. "It's Ira Judelson."

The guy went off. "I know who the fuck it is. You still bothering me about the fucking money? I'm living in the street. I put up my son's house. And you're bothering me about the fucking money. I'll cut your fuckin' throat, ear to ear, you cocksucking Jew motherfucker."

The guy was practically spitting into the phone, he'd whipped himself into such a complete frenzy, and I was thrown, taken aback. I was sitting in my office, and I remember hanging up the phone, wondering if I should be scared of this guy. I was nervous, shook up, but I had to think this guy was just venting, blowing smoke. Still, I didn't know what to do. I wasn't afraid of a fight. I don't care if you're six-five, with muscles and tattoos, I'll scrap with you any day of the week. I don't give a shit. Even if I take a beating, I don't give a shit. But this was a made guy—a well-known associate of an alleged mob family—and he was really, really laying into me. I'd been called a lot of things, but nobody'd ever called me a cocksucking Jew motherfucker, so I reached out to Murray to get his take.

There's a reason they called this guy Don't Worry Murray—not *just* because he took good care of his clients, but because nothing seemed to rattle him. He's got a way about him, Murray Richman, leaves everyone else thinking things will shake out just fine—and they usually do, only here this turned out not to be the case. I told Murray who I was calling about, and he stopped me before I could tell him the story. "Ira, I don't represent him anymore. He couldn't pay me."

"You, too? He won't pay me, either." Then I told Murray the rest of the story, told him how I was into the insurance company on this.

By the end of the call, Murray told me he'd look into it, see what he could do, and he called back a couple days later with the name of the associate's new attorney, so I got this guy on the phone and told him the story.

"Ira, tell me what you want me to do," the attorney said when I was finished.

I asked him to reach out to the alleged captain, fill him in on my problem, see if maybe he could intercede, smooth things over.

Next day, I got a call from the alleged captain. He didn't want to talk at length on the phone, so we arranged a place to meet—at the Odyssey Diner, in Eastchester, New York. At midnight, no less.

The meet sounded like a setup, but a part of me knew it wasn't a setup. It was just how these guys did business, so I went along, said I'd meet him there, no problem. Before I left for the meeting, though, I called the lawyer again to get his take. I said, "Tommy, I'm not gonna get killed here, am I?"

"Probably not, but you never know." He was a real joker, this one.

Still, I didn't think I'd get whacked over $15,000, so I wasn't too worried. Only reason I was even a little bit worried was because of my young family. Ava was a little over two years old and Blake was very, very pregnant with Casey. On top of that, we were getting ready to move into a new house, a three-bedroom town house in Rye Brook, so a lot of stuff was going on. I couldn't afford to have this guy cut my fuckin' throat, ear to ear.

Blake was pretty emotional when I laid it all out for her. "Let it go, Ira. It's just seventy-five hundred dollars to you after the insurance."

"I can't let it go, Blake. One thing, it's not just seventy-five to me. It's the full fifteen thousand. I'll have to make it right with the insurance company, so I'm out their cut, too."

But it wasn't just the money, of course. I explained to Blake that if I pulled my pants down on this, it would get around that this was shit that could be pulled on me. It would be the end of me in this business—which, after all, is a business of relationships. "I can't show any weakness on this."

"Isn't there someone you can call?" she asked. A reasonable question.

Truth was, I had a "rabbi" in the business—my buddy Ralph, who'd always helped me navigate these mob-related waters. He knew everyone, everything, but I couldn't call on him anymore. Why? Because he'd "disappeared" a couple years back. Obviously I couldn't tell Blake about this because it would just confirm her fears, so I just told her there was no one to call. "Trust me on this, Blake," I said, hoping to end the conversation. "I know how to take care of myself."

She argued, quite reasonably, that this wasn't any kind of fair fight. "It's not like you're using your hands. These are sick people. At least bring a gun."

"Blake, I can't bring a gun. I'm going to a meet, in a public place, with an alleged captain. If I bring a gun, I'll get killed."

She was so emotional, so pregnant, I don't know why I put her through all of this. Looking back, I realize I should probably have just gone off to the meeting without saying anything, but we needed to go over a couple things. I needed to tell her where I was going, exactly. Who I was meeting with, exactly. Who to call and what to do if I didn't check in with her, exactly.

The diner was only fifteen minutes from my house, but I left at about eleven fifteen. I wanted to get there early, way early, hang in the parking lot, listen to the sports-radio station, and see who was coming and going. Finally, I went inside, asked to use the bathroom. Checked the place out as thoroughly as I could, looking for anything suspicious. Went back outside, listened to the radio some more.

At about eleven fifty-five, a car pulled up—the alleged captain. He appeared to be alone. He got out of his car and went inside. I followed him in about five minutes later, saw he had a cup of coffee already in front of him.

He motioned to the booth, other side of the table from him. "Kid, sit down. You wanna eat something?"

"I'm good. Not even hungry."

"Coffee?"

I shook him off in a no-thanks way. Then I went right into it. I told him I had a little problem with his well-known associate. I told him the problem, and he listened so carefully it looked like he was taking notes in his head, wanting to remember every detail.

"So he owes you fifteen thousand, right?" he asked when I was finished.

I nodded.

The alleged captain, he seemed to think about this for a while—long enough I started to think I should have ordered something to eat.

I couldn't stand the silence, so I said, "I did this on spec, out of respect for you and your family. I'm out-of-pocket with the insurance company. I haven't seen a dime."

Across the table, the alleged captain was apparently still gathering his thoughts, so I continued, building up a head of steam, "And if I don't get paid on this, I'll never bail out anyone in your family ever again."

It surprised me that I'd make such a bold, ballsy pronouncement, but it just came out of me—and soon as it did, I regretted it.

The alleged captain flashed me a look that told me I was pushing it, so I dialed things down. I thought, No sense pissing this guy off unless I have to—and right now, I didn't have to, not yet.

The alleged captain seemed to chew on this for a beat. "Listen, kid," he finally said. "I don't want to see you get beat. Will you settle for ten?" Meaning, would I accept sixty-six cents on the dollar.

"If I owed $150,000 gambling, would you take $100,000?" I said, putting my answer back to him in the form of a question, like I was on *Jeopardy!* and not playing with my life.

Again, the alleged captain flashed me the look, and for the first time that night I stopped to think just who I was dealing with. This guy was notorious. The stories had him taking baseball bats to people when they stepped out of line. He'd made his bones the hard way, had a couple bodies on the street . . . all of that. Wasn't smart, me pushing up on him like this, but I didn't see any other way to play it. I had to come at this guy from a position of strength—otherwise, my whole business was screwed.

"You'll have your money," he said finally.

"Thank you, sir."

"Okay if I piece it off to you?" Meaning, the street version of an installment plan.

"No problem."

"One thing, though. Not a word." Meaning, to the well-known associate.

I nodded.

Two days later, a kid came to my office—a bag boy, I guessed. Handed me an envelope with $4,000. A week later, $3,000. The next week, $2,600. After four or five weeks, I was paid in full.

Meanwhile, the well-known associate was *shelved*—a lovely little euphemism in the family business for losing your button. It means you're no longer made, no longer protected, so it's like open season on your ass. This came clear to me over the next year or so, as this well-known *former* associate's case went to trial. Took a couple years to play out in court, and when it was over, the guy called me at my office to settle the paperwork. He spoke with the same brass and bluster he'd shown in the beginning—because, hey, the guy had no idea I knew he was on the shelf.

"You gotta release my kid's house."

"Who the hell is this?" I knew who the hell this was, but I wanted to bust his chops.

He gave me his name. "My case is over. You need to take care of this for me."

I explained that he needed to go to the courthouse and get a disposition, allowing me to release the lien on his son's house.

"You can do that. That's why I fuckin' paid you."

"No, I'm not doing that. It's not my job."

"Who the fuck do you think you're talkin' to?"

"Me?" I said. "Who the fuck do *I* think I'm talkin' to? Who the fuck do *you* think you're talkin' to, you cocksucking mother-fucker?"

Then I hung up on him—and it felt great. This piece of shit, he couldn't touch me. He was just a regular civilian, same as me.

Word got around, how I talked to this guy. In some circles, it's like I was a legend, how I talked to this guy. In others, it's like this well-known *former* associate was a joke, how he let a guy like *me* talk to a guy like *him*. Either way, word got all the way around to the alleged captain, who called me up to chew me out. He said, "I thought I told you to keep your mouth shut on this."

"I'm sorry, sir. But I didn't tell him our arrangement. I just told him off."

"And why was it necessary to do that?"

"I might be a lot of things. Who knows, I might even be a cocksucking motherfucker, as your friend suggested. But nobody calls me a cocksucking Jew motherfucker and gets away with it."

•    •    •

My youngest, Charlie, was born in 2008—fat in the middle of yet another huge corruption case. This third time, with our daughter Charlie . . . well, it was weird and a little wacky the way *all* of our birth and delivery stories were stacked up alongside these dozens of bails, involving most of New York's crime families.

We'd since moved from the town house in Rye Brook to the house where we currently live, so our lives, like my business, were getting bigger, more complicated. And this case was turning out to be one of the biggest, most complicated of my career. I'd already written about twelve bails that day before Blake went into labor. I was cranking, plowing through all the paperwork, because I knew Blake was about to burst and I wanted to get these bails done. Six defendants were already out the door, all made guys or well-known associates, but the other six were held up with surety hearings. The DA had a right to examine our bail packages, make sure the money wasn't dirty, but it felt to me like overkill. The defendants might have been dirty—or at least their "associates" might have been known to be dirty—but the bails were good, the money clean.

I knew I had to be in court the next morning to clear these bails. Wasn't an option, me telling the judge I had to step away because my wife was giving birth. Wasn't an option for a lot of reasons, but mostly because I liked things to go well when I was working for this particular clientele. Do it right, and you'll earn yourself a ton of business going forward. Mess it up, and you'll get the kind of headache that doesn't always go away. And it's not like there was anyone in my office I could have sent instead of me—or, at least, not like I was about to trust someone else with such an important task. Yeah, we were in good shape on these bail packages, but I still needed them to be processed swiftly, and for that I'd need a little help from the court. *That* kind of help I was willing to accept, only it wasn't so easy to come by. For every kind and decent judge like the Honorable Jeffrey Atlas, who'd thrown me a wink and a bone right after the birth of my daughter Ava, there was a pain-in-the-ass like the one assigned to this case, who'd bury me and my clients if I wasn't available on his schedule—or, in this case, who'd drag his feet just to see me sit and stew.

With any luck, I'd get all these guys out before Blake went into labor. Otherwise, we were screwed.

Sure enough, Blake woke up at four o'clock the next morning, feeling like it was time. "If I even move, I'm gonna go into labor," she said. So I sat her down on the couch, in some type of yoga position, and stayed with her for a couple hours, trying to keep her calm. By eight o'clock, she thought the contractions were under control, thought she could make it to the end of the day— at least, judging by how things had gone with the two previous pregnancies—so I raced to my office in Queens to get a jump start, hoping to get these defendants out the door before Charlie came barreling out the door.

And that's nearly how it shook out—but *nearly* doesn't always cut it.

I spent the morning with the DA—a good, good guy, saw right away what I was up against. "You gotta do me a favor," I said. "My wife's about to give birth. These bails are good. The money's clean. Go over the paperwork, see for yourself, but whatever you can do to speed this along, I'd appreciate it."

The DA looked over the paperwork double-quick, said he could approve five of the packages, but he had a couple questions on the sixth. The other cases had all been approved, too—but they were mostly cash bonds, so those guys were already out. This sixth remaining case, though, looked like it might jack me up, take a while. Finally, I was able to put it in decent-enough shape that the DA could sign off on it, and we raced the cases over to the courthouse, hoping to get them in and heard and done before lunch. Didn't exactly happen that way, though. The DA stood in front of the judge and said, "Your Honor, I'm waiving all the sureties in this case." Meaning the hearings he was entitled to request to check on our money. He also told the judge that my wife was about to go into labor—maybe appeal to this guy's sense of decency and humanity, get him to speed things along.

So what happened? The dick judge sat on his hands for the next hour while he dealt with a mess of other shit on his calendar—in a way that felt to me like he was just making me wait, just because he had the power to do so. I had to bite my tongue to keep from making a scene. Finally, a couple minutes before one o'clock, the judge called our case and we got all the bails done, and I sprinted down the hallway and out the door to my car. I'd had my phone in my pocket the whole time because I didn't want to piss off this dick judge any more than I apparently had, and as I ran for the exit, I flipped it open to check for messages. I saw a couple missed calls from Blake's cell phone, hit REDIAL.

My wife's friend Jen picked up. "Ira, we couldn't wait."

"You're at the hospital?"

"Yes."

"Greenwich Hospital?" Making sure.

"Yes."

I tore off in the direction of the Triborough Bridge, ignoring the speed limit, the traffic, everything. Naturally, I got pulled over, so I showed the cop this special badge I carry, which sometimes gets law enforcement to look the other way. Not this guy, though. He was by-the-book, the whole way—the traffic-cop version of the dick judge I'd faced earlier. "Where you going in such a hurry, Mr. Judelson?"

I told him my wife was about to go into labor, and I was trying to get to the hospital to meet her.

"Still, you were going eighty miles an hour."

"Look, my man, either the ticket or the lecture, not both."

He settled on the ticket—and he took his sweet time writing it out. "You know, Mr. Judelson," he said, when he finally came back to my window and handed it to me, "I was planning to let this one slide, but I didn't like your attitude."

I took the ticket. "Yeah, well, you can wipe your fuckin' ass with this ticket."

It wasn't the most elegant or professional response, but it's what I came up with at the time. Then I sped away—not quite at eighty miles an hour, but fast enough to kind of flip this guy off.

Blake was in the delivery room when I arrived, two thirty or so, not quite in full-blown labor but getting there. She was pissed at me for not being home to take her to the hospital, but soon she was in too much pain for that. But she'd be pissed at me again, soon enough. We still had to cut through some bureaucracy on these bails before my defendants could walk, so I had my phone to my ear the whole time I was in the delivery room.

By seven, seven thirty, Blake was back to being completely, totally pissed at me. She was screaming, in full-blown labor. The nurses had her legs up in stirrups—one leg in Ohio, the other in Michigan. Me, I was hovering up around Blake's head, trying not to get hit when she flailed her arms and lashed out in pain, and at the same time letting her grab on to me, dig her nails into me, tug at my hair . . . whatever she needed to transfer her agony and frustration onto me. But then my phone went off, right in the middle of a killer contraction, and Blake turned to me with a look of fury.

"Don't you fuckin' pick up that phone!"

I peaked at the phone's display window, recognized a Rikers Island number. "Blake, honey, I've got to take this."

"I'm serious, Ira. Don't you fuckin' pick up that fuckin' phone!"

At just that moment, I couldn't think which was more terrifying—to go against the rage and fury of these mobbed-up guys at Rikers, or to go against the rage and fury of my wife, in full-blown labor. I was fucked either way . . . so I picked up the phone, figured with Blake at least I stood a decent chance of making repairs.

It was one of my defendants—another well-known associate whose brother was the reputed consigliere of a major crime family. My client was a heavy-duty guy, a made guy, and I wanted things to go right for him, here on in—because if things went right for him, they'd go right for me. But I could hardly hear him, through the commotion of the delivery room, through Blake's screams, through whatever was happening on his end of the phone at Rikers.

"Ira, am I getting out? What's taking so long?" There was no panic in his voice—rather, he sounded insistent, matter-of-fact, like he expected nothing less than his immediate release and was just trying to understand the timetable.

"It can take a while. Just hang in there." I told him I couldn't talk, told him I was in the delivery room with my wife—but he might have figured that out for himself from the way Blake was yelling in the background.

She was saying things like "Tell him to go fuck himself!" "You and your asshole mob friends!" "Hang up the fuckin' phone, you piece of shit!"

Probably, this well-known associate, this brother of a reputed consigliere, wasn't used to people talking to him in just this way. He said, "So, like, tonight? I'm getting out tonight?"

"That's the plan. Next couple hours." Here I was trying to reassure my client, the whole time knowing I was digging myself a deep, deep hole with my wife, but I didn't see any other way to play it.

It was impossible for this guy *not* to hear what was going on in the delivery room, and he laughed and finally said something about it. "Sounds like you got your hands full, Ira."

"You got that right, my man."

For years afterward, after this guy went in, he'd call to check in and say, "How's my kid?" A little creepy, but kinda sweet. I told him Blake and I thought about naming our daughter after him, and he laughed and laughed like this was the funniest fucking thing in the world.

And it was—only Blake didn't think it was so funny. Even now, she won't laugh, except in a kind of grudging way, because to her my refusal to shut off my cell phone at such a powerful, personal moment in our lives was an indication of my commitment to our family—or, I should say, to my *lack* of commitment. But that wasn't the case at all, and it took Blake a while to come around to my way of thinking on this. It's still a constant source of agitation between us, the way I'm always "working," always on the phone, but she gets that I'm obsessive about my business. And she gets that I have to be obsessive if I want to keep my edge.

I had to go at this business all out, all the time, because if I wasn't there to pick up the phone when someone needed me to write a bail, they'd call the next bondsman on the list. Didn't matter if my wife was in labor. Didn't matter if my kids kept popping out, one after the other, in the fat middle of the biggest corruption scandals of the decade.

Work was work. And that was that.

# 6

# What to Do When the Shit Goes Down

In my world, everyone who walks in the door is innocent. It's not for me to tell them they're full of shit—but, hey, the DA's office doesn't push a case unless there's *something*. Nobody's 100 percent innocent, 100 percent of the time—not me, not you . . . not even your blessed mother. (No offense.) We're all guilty of something, and if you're jammed up and looking at time, you're probably guilty of way more than you're letting on.

Nine times out of ten, by the time a case gets to me, there's something to it. Might even be ninety-nine times out of a hundred. The numbers don't exactly tilt in my clients' favor, but that doesn't mean I can't help them out.

How it goes down is usually like this: I'll get an urgent call from a wife or a parent or some close friend or family member.

Sometimes the call will come directly from the defendant. They'll tell me they got my name from their attorney, from a flyer they picked up outside the courtroom, from the storefront-type sign just outside one of my offices. They'll tell me bail has been set at $5,000, $50,000, $500,000 . . . whatever the number is, it feels pretty damn big. Funny how that works. Judge sets a bail, he comes up with a number that means something. Not so big that it's pie-in-the-sky, hopelessly out of reach, and not so small that it's right there in the pocket already.

The number's got to be just right. It's got to fit the crime and the circumstances both. It's got to hurt—or else the defendant will walk. But it's also got to help—because if it can't get the defendant out the door, then what the hell's the point?

First question I always ask is "What were you arrested for?"

Then I have a long list of follow-ups:

"Have you ever been arrested before?"

"Do you have any priors?" As in, prior convictions.

"Who's bailing you out?"

"How big is the bond?"

"What do you have for collateral?"

"Are you a US citizen?"

First couple answers are always the tell. Typically, I'll hear back that the person has been arrested but never did time. But not always. If the person's done time, it can be a good sign or a bad sign, depending. Good, because it tells me the person knows what it means to be incarcerated. He understands what it is to do time. Bad, because it means he's a repeat offender—first time around, for whatever reason, the punishment didn't exactly do the job.

The body language, too, gives each client away—the way someone leans when he talks, the way he looks at me or looks away, the way he strings his words together . . . there's another whole bunch of tells.

If I don't like what I hear, if I don't like what I see, I don't do the bond. For the most part, I stay away from noncitizens. These days, that's a nonstarter for me—a giant red flag. Why? It's too easy for them to jump bail because they have a place to go—friends and family back home who might close ranks and make the flight risk a little too much for me to want to take on. They'll disappear on me, disappear back into their old lives, and I'll be stuck with the bond.

(That's an elastic rule—meaning, I stretch it from time to time—but I do so at my own peril.)

I also avoid two-time predicate felons—meaning, guys who have already been convicted of two felonies at two different times. Most judges have a three-strikes-and-you're-out rule, which means the two-timers are looking at serious time, which in turn means they've got all the more reason to duck out on a bail. You're in the system this deep, you know how it works, and here it works against you—again, a little too much incentive for this potential client to leave me hanging.

(It's another rule I can bend and stretch to help me make an argument for or against, even though I know better than to take up the *for* side of the argument.)

Just because someone's done time, it's not necessarily a knock. Mostly, it's a caution. There's a saying in and around the criminal justice system: "Everybody's up to do the crime, but nobody wants to do the time." Only here it tells me this guy is willing to *lay down*—meaning, he knows what it is to be held accountable, knows there's life after prison, long as he doesn't fuck it up and wind up back in the system.

I ask the same questions as every other bail bondsman in town. The difference comes in how we respond to the answers, to all these different tells. Like I said, when I was just starting out, I took a lot of chances. I was hungry to make a name for myself, to make a splash in the business. Also, I needed the money. I had a payroll to meet, office expenses, a young family to support—so I made some bad decisions, got beat on a lot of bad bails. Lately, I've become way more conservative. I've still got all those expenses—in fact, my nut has only gotten *bigger* over the years—but now there's more of a cushion. Now there's a track record, a hard-earned reputation, so I'll stay away from a bond if it looks like it might burn me. That's not because I've changed my nature, but my needs have changed. Now I come at each bond from a different place, with the mind-set that I have everything to lose, where before I took more of an everything-to-gain approach.

Might seem like a small shift, but the difference is everything.

Generally speaking, there's a bail for every bondsman. Even if I pass on a case, another bondsman in town will take it. And chances are, a lot of the cases I end up taking have been passed over by someone else who might have seen too many holes. One man's bad bet is another man's payday—and like I said, I took on a lot of those dicey bonds early on. But a lot of times when a guy looks like too much of a flight risk, when there's no collateral, no compelling family ties to keep him from jumping, nobody wants to take a bail, and when that happens, the defendant is shit out of luck. Just because a judge sets bail and determines a defendant is not a flight risk, is not a danger to society, or even that it would cost the city or the state too much to incarcerate him while the case goes to trial, it doesn't mean we're obligated to post a bond.

It just means the defendant is *eligible*—and last I checked, *eligible* and *entitled* don't exactly mean the same thing.

On *eligible*, the judge gets to decide. On *entitled*, it falls to the bondsman—so it's not like I'm any kind of jury, deciding who gets to walk. No, I'm just looking to cover my ass.

A lot of folks, they turn on the television, they get an idea what we do, how we do it. On a show like *Law & Order*, they've got the procedural part down pretty good. But those shows don't go much deeper than that. It's just the broad strokes. They don't show how a defendant's family can be ripped apart by a criminal case, how they're coming to someone like me at a vulnerable time. Hey, it can be the worst time of their lives, the bottom of the bottom. To some families, it feels like they're about to lose everything.

Sometimes, I'll hear from a wife, and she's been instructed by her husband in prison to put up their house as collateral, but she can't find the deed. Maybe she doesn't pay the bills, maybe she's got no idea how much the home is worth, what her monthly mortgage payments might be. You'd think the bank could be some help on this, but at times a defendant's assets are frozen and the bank is unable to cooperate.

Also, on television, they don't go much below the surface. If you hear that a house is worth, say, $250,000, that's about as far as it goes. The rest of the story turns on these same round numbers, to where it starts to feel like a game of Monopoly—you know, a property is worth a precise number, and buying and selling properties is as easy as rolling the dice. But that's not how it works. In the real world, in *my* world, a house might be worth $250,000 on the market, but I've got to take that number and figure out what it's worth to me. I'm not playing Monopoly. I'm not in the real estate business. I don't have time to stake a FOR SALE sign in the front yard and wait around for the best offer. I don't want to be on the hook for the 6 percent agent's commission, or to deal with all the paperwork and closing costs that bite you in the ass when you buy or sell a house. Who needs that shit? Not me, so when I take a $250,000 piece of property as collateral, I factor all of that in. I think in worst-case scenarios. I ask myself what the property would be worth if I had to sell it immediately, after taking out all these other costs, so it might end up that it's only worth $195,000, in real terms.

Folks don't like to hear that when I put it back on them, but I'm in this business to make money, not friends. And the only way I *make* money is by protecting my money. I'm lending it out—so, hell yeah, I want to make sure I get it back.

I subscribe to a service called PropertyShark, tells me instantly what a piece of property is worth on a short sale. It gives me a whole range, but I take a conservative number. Also, I have a lawyer on retainer who oversees my paperwork on deeds, and I'm a partner in an abstract company that runs title searches on houses, researches deeds, arranges transfer documents, so I'm set up in a bunch of different ways to keep these pain-in-the-ass administrative costs down—but they're still a pain in the ass, and I try to factor that in.

Same deal with jewelry. I'll see someone with a $25,000 Rolex, and an appraisal to prove it's legit, but I know that if I have to sell that watch in a heartbeat, I'd only get half that number. Diamonds, pearls, gold . . . the stuff's got sentimental value to these people, too, but I've got no time for sentimental value. I take in a piece of jewelry like I'd have to fence it tomorrow—meaning, sell it on the street with a gun to my head. When you have to sell, it cuts into your leverage, and that brings the number way, way down. Here, too, I've got a buddy in the pawn business I know I can trust, but I don't give people dollar for dollar on their jewelry. I can't. Still, people hear that, they get all bent out of shape. "No disrespect, Mr. Judelson," they say, "but that watch is worth twenty-five thousand dollars." And I'll shoot back, "No disrespect, but it's not worth twenty-five thousand dollars to *me*."

When they want to put up a business, I have to look at the books. I have to look at the property. The lease, the equipment, the goods . . . and I've got to tell you, this shit drives me plain crazy. (What do I know from receivables?) If I wanted to go into the pizza business or the dry-cleaning business, I would have done it on my own. To do it on the back of a bad bond makes no sense, so I try to steer clear of these types of deals.

It's crazy, some of the shit I've been offered as collateral. Real estate, furs, jewelry, boats, cars and recreational vehicles, stocks and bonds . . . the usual. But I've also had people offer to babysit my kids or service my car or clean my office. One guy actually sat across from my desk and pulled a gold tooth out of his mouth—and I remember thinking, What the hell am I supposed to do with *that*? Every time I take on a prostitution case, I half-expect the suspect to offer me a blow job or a couple throws with one of her colleagues, but that hasn't happened yet.

Folks have an inflated sense of what their property is worth, what their goods and services are worth, and I have to think defensively, so I guess that means I have a deflated sense. At times we're so far apart I can't even get close to doing a bond. A family might come to me seeking a million-dollar bail, and they can only scrape together a half million in assets, but I might want to help them out anyway. When that happens, I'll try to work with them—only it's not like I'm about to cover them on that half-million-dollar difference. No, this is where I put on my *macher* hat and try to help them work out a new deal. I'll give them the benefit of the doubt *and* the benefit of my experience. Add those two benefits together and maybe I can get my client to consider wearing a monitoring bracelet, or maybe make some other appeal to a judge to get him to reduce the bond.

I'll give them the benefit of my experience, my relationships. The bracelet helps. I've had families in tears because they can only put together a bail package totaling less than half the number on the bond, and everyone's just distraught because it's looking more and more like Junior will have to sit and stew in prison while his case snakes its way to trial. But maybe I like the kid, or I like the family, and I get the feeling that these are good people caught in a tough spot, so I'll talk to them about going back to the judge. Happens all the time. I'll meet with their attorney, who might be new to this type of case, suggest they tell the judge Junior would be willing to wear an ankle bracelet, maybe work out some type of home confinement. Set it up so the kid can still go back and forth to work, maybe back and forth to church, back and forth to the doctor . . . whatever. Sometimes, I'll even go before the judge and show him how the GPS tracking device in the bracelet works, and the judge will consider the appeal, consider the case in a new way—and half the time he'll come back with a lower number. Might not be the number this family can afford, but it gets them closer to it—and, who knows, maybe it gets me closer to taking a little bit more of a chance. Every once in a while, a judge might ask for some additional element in our bail package—like maybe he'll want the defendant to surrender his passport—and this also goes a long way in bringing down the size of the bond.

When you connect with a client or his family, you fix it so these people can get their lives back to how they were—at least until the court says otherwise.

When you don't, and the numbers don't make sense, you walk away.

It's not *just* about the bond, what I do. Yeah, that's where it always starts, but sometimes it's not even *mostly* about the bond. It's everything else besides.

A couple years back, I did a bail for a kid named Eric—a young guy pinched in a big credit-card/identity scam. Kid had a ring going where he was stealing people's information from credit-card slips in restaurants, so they jacked him up. Call came in saying this was a "good" guy from a "good" family caught in a bad, bad way—a typical white-collar crime in a city like New York.

Like always, I didn't give a shit what he may or may not have done, long as he had property to back up the bond, long as he wasn't going anywhere. The wrinkle here was that Eric's wife was pregnant at the time of his arrest—like, superpregnant, because she ended up giving birth while Eric was being arrested and arraigned, which left it so he didn't even get to see his baby being born. All of that added a little bit of urgency to the case because obviously Eric wanted to get out and get home to see his wife and kid.

I ended up doing the bail for a pretty big number. Worked with the guy's father. He actually came to my home, the dad. Spent a lot of time putting the package together because on a larceny case the surety hearings can be a bitch. Court looks long and hard to make sure the money is clean—and here we had to go out of our way to prove it.

During that surety process, I became pretty tight with the ADA on the case—and I mention this piece only because it set up what happened next.

All that time, I never met with my client. I might have spoken to Eric on the phone a time or two, congratulated him on his new family, told him I was working hard for him, but we were never in the same room together. Yet even on the phone, I decided I didn't like this guy. There was just something about him, you know. He came at me, each conversation, like the world had done him dirt, like the system was lined up against him. Didn't seem to *own* that he'd maybe brought this shitstorm on himself.

All my dealings were with his father, and eventually we got Eric out. Clearly, it was an important time in their lives, and I remember how grateful Eric was to be going home. Not as grateful as his father, not as grateful as his wife, but grateful enough. He went out of his way to let me know, which was something. Still didn't like this kid all that much, but at least he knew to show his appreciation.

After that, I kind of put the case out of my mind, which is how it usually happens. I've got so many open bails, so many cases pending, there's no way I could track each and every one. My head would explode. Instead, like I've said, all these little checks and balances are built into our office systems, allowing me to track each case as it goes to trial . . . so after a couple months, I'd pretty much forgotten about Eric.

Next thing I knew, I got a call from a buddy of mine, who happened to be a friend of Eric's. We'd never made the connection, but I heard from this mutual friend telling me Eric wanted to reach out. Said Eric was going to take a plea—meaning, he'd plead guilty to a lesser charge—and that he wanted to talk to me.

My buddy wanted to know if it was okay for him to give Eric my cell phone number.

I figured, Hey, what the hell do I care, this kid calls me on my cell or at the office? It was all the same to me. "Sure, tell him to call," I said.

Meanwhile, I got another call, from *another* buddy who was also friendly with Eric. I thought, Man, this guy's got friends all over the place—friends of *mine* all over the place. Once again, I said it was cool to give Eric my number.

Everyone knows someone—and I'd been at this long enough I know just about everyone. For me, it's about due diligence. It comes into play when I try to help out a mom worried about her son, wanting to make his time go easier. She might come to me to see what I can do, and I reach back to friends, former clients, grasping at whatever strings I can pull. And it gets around, that I'm wired in this way.

These two buddies of mine, it's like they were double-teaming me on this one.

Finally, Eric called. Started telling me he was innocent, how the DA was putting the squeeze on his wife, who may or may not have been involved in this identity-theft scam, pressuring him to take this deal and plead guilty to the larceny charge. He was anxious about doing time—scared shitless. Said he'd heard from his friends that I was a good guy to know, maybe I could make a couple calls.

Don't know what it was, but something about this guy still rubbed me wrong. It had been almost a year since we did the bail, but as soon as I heard his voice, other end of the phone, it came back to me. Maybe it was the way he was proclaiming his innocence, all the time talking about how he was about to cop a plea.

Maybe it was how he made me feel like he was touching me up for a favor he didn't exactly have coming.

Anyway, he laid it all out for me. "Ira, man, you do this for me, I'll be your friend for life."

Again, don't know why, but his approach kind of set me off. "I have enough friends," I said.

"You don't understand. I'm a good guy. I didn't do what they're saying."

"I know, I know. You're innocent. Everyone's innocent." Like I didn't have time for this shit.

I was hard on this kid, but after I smacked him around for a while on the phone I told him I'd help him out. "I'm not doing this for you. I don't want your friendship. I'm doing this for my buddies. For some reason, they've vouched for you, they've asked me to help, so I'll help."

First move I made was to try to get Eric's wife off the case. This was where that good relationship with the ADA came back in. I called the guy up, laid it all out for him. I wanted to know if Eric could fall on his own sword, maybe take some of the heat off his wife.

"Listen, Ira," the ADA said, "you're trying to do the right thing here. The wife just had a baby. I can't tell you what we've got on her, but it wouldn't hurt, maybe this kid writes a letter to the judge."

So I got Eric to write a letter to the judge—helped him on it, too. Told him just what to say, threw in just the right amount of remorse, regret, responsibility . . . whatever.

And it worked—seemed to, anyway. The DA backed off on the wife, let Eric cop to an additional charge or two, which set it up for Eric to do his time. Ended up pleading out to grand larceny two. Judge gave him two to six years, which was about what the kid deserved, only now he started freaking out about stepping in. That's what they call it when you start your bid. *Stepping in*—as in, the moment you step inside the joint. Makes it sound like you're crossing a threshold to a kick-ass party, instead of shedding your freedom, your dignity, your sense of self-worth and self-control.

Here I had a different set of buddies I wanted to give an assist to—two friends of mine, ex-cons, who'd just started a prison consultation business. Between them, they'd done forty years. Between them, they'd served time in over twenty different facilities. They knew the system inside out and upside down, figured they could make a business coaching kids like Eric through their bid for a nice fee.

All around New York—all around the country—you're starting to see these types of consultants. My thinking: this is a good thing all around. They provide a real service, so here I thought I could make a nice referral to my ex-con pals, and at the same time do a solid for my other two pals who'd vouched for Eric in the first place. And me doing right by my buddies, Eric would also benefit, so it was a win-win all around.

The right prison consultant, he'll set you up. He'll help you understand the lay of the land inside—how to move, how to talk, what to expect. But even more than that, he can help you with your commissary, make sure you get the clothes you need, maybe a radio or a television, maybe some special privileges. He doesn't just know the system, he know's the people—*specific* people. My guys had only been out a short time, so they were still wired to guards *and* prisoners in a position to help my client's bid go easy.

The ex-cons were thrilled with the referral because they were *just* starting out, and this was one of their first cases. They weren't even sure how much to charge, how much their clients would pay, that's how *new* this business was for them. Eric was thrilled, too, because he was really, really sweating it out. He was assigned to a facility where one of my buddies had served, so they were able to direct him to a heavy hitter on the inside who'd see that Eric's bid went easy. Gave Eric the guy's name, his cellblock number, said to write and introduce himself. So that's what Eric did—only before he heard back from the gangbanger, I got a call from one of my prison consultant pals: "Ira, man, this kid Eric, we'll help him out, he's a client, but he's gotta learn to keep his mouth shut. Talks a lot, this one."

Already, Eric was rubbing these guys the wrong way—same way he was rubbing me the wrong way. Like I said, there was just something about him, and it followed him inside. Still, it was business, so my guys set him up with the VIP treatment. Saw that he was protected. Saw that he had a new pair of sneakers, home-cooked meals, money in his commissary account, some dudes to walk the yard with . . . whatever. He was all set—but he set people off.

After a couple weeks, word came back to me through these two prison consultants that Eric was a jerk on the ward—you know, like a blowhard. But the gangbanger still had Eric's back, as a favor to the gangbanger's prison consultant pal—and, no doubt, for some kind of kickback. And the prison consultants still had Eric's back because they didn't think they'd get their consulting business off the ground if they worried too much about actually *liking* their clients, and because they wanted to do right by me—which I thought was kind of ironic because the only reason I'd stuck my neck out for this kid was my friendship with our two mutual pals, and I'd wanted to do right by *them.*

But that's how it goes sometimes. The bond itself was a good piece of business. Everything else, it was a chance to parcel out a couple favors, spread some goodwill to folks who could maybe help me a little further down the road.

It's all part of the same job.


It's a fucked-up system, but it's the only system we've got, so I find a way to make it work. Like I said, in my world, everyone's innocent. Only thing folks are guilty of is maybe being in the wrong place at the wrong time. Of being up against it when an easy way around presents itself.

But then you start to listen to my clients' stories, and you hear how good people can get into bad places. How good people can make mistakes. Even how good people can sometimes get railroaded by a cop, a DA, a judge, out to build a career on the back of someone's misstep.

Happens all the time—and when it does, it falls to me to bail people out in what ways I know.

So what do you do when you're jammed up? Who do you call if a friend or family member is on the wrong side of a bad day, looking at time? What if it's you in a shit pile of trouble?

Doesn't much matter if you're guilty or innocent, straight out of the gate. What matters is getting your ass out of jail, making sure things go easy—at least, as easy as possible, depending on the depth of your shit pile. What matters is making sure you don't do anything stupid, on top of all the other stupid things you may or may not have done to land your ass in the joint in the first place.

One of my sideline businesses is a website and a mobile phone application designed to help folks out in just this way—www

.JammedUp.com. (Cool name, huh?) Forgive, please, the blatant product placement—but, hey, I'm a hustler at heart. This app and the website tie in to one of the takeaways of this book. They're set up to be the go-to resource when you're "in a jam"—one-stop shopping for anyone facing criminal charges or seeking help navigating the twists and turns of the criminal justice system. We offer references and guidance on virtually all legal issues, including civil litigation, landlord-tenant disputes, fraud and negligence cases, custody battles, and traffic violations, but my area of expertise is the full range of criminal charges, so I hook people up with specific information organized by state and local municipalities. I also lay on some straight-shooting advice on how to carry yourself on the inside, and how to keep your time inside to a minimum, if that's what it comes down to.

So, in the "jammed up" spirit, here's a handy checklist of what to do (and what not to do) if the shit ever hits the fan:

**DON'T HANG OUT WITH GARBAGE**—probably the single best piece of advice I can offer. You are who you associate with, and if you spend your time hanging with gangbangers and punks, you'll get caught in the same swirl. I don't care if you're a choirboy at heart, if your friends are out there kicking up some dust, some of that dust will attach to you. So choose your friends wisely. Don't put yourself in a bad position. If you smell a fight brewing, walk away—trust me, it's not gonna end up good. You'll be stuck with a $50,000 legal bill, or a $100,000 bail bond, or possible state-prison time. Be smart.

**DO PAY YOUR PARKING TICKETS**—and keep your registration current. This falls under that same "be smart" category, and it applies if you're already in the system or if you're otherwise squeaky-clean. You'd be amazed how many first-time offenders get pulled over for a simple traffic violation (running a red light, a busted taillight . . . whatever), and then when the cop runs the plates, he turns up a whole mess of trouble. Folks go from looking at a fine or maybe a suspended license to jail time, all on the back of some unpaid tickets.

**DON'T DRIVE WITHOUT YOUR LICENSE**—no need to give a police officer a reason to jack you up, so keep your license and registration handy. Always, always, always. If for some reason this is a problem for you, take the time to make copies and keep them in your glove compartment. A current copy, with legit driver and vehicle IDs, will at least buy you some time or some goodwill if you're pulled over without the real deal.

**DO TRY TO BE COURTEOUS AND RESPECTFUL**—at all times, with any arresting officer, court officer, prison guard . . . up and down the chain of custody. Give someone a reason to do you dirt and he surely will. Give someone a reason to do you a solid and he just might.

**DON'T "BLOW"**—a final tip in the traffic-stop category, this one comes into play if you're pulled over on a suspected DWI: under no circumstances should you submit to a Breathalyzer test in the field. There are so many ways to get around the calibration and beat the test in court, it's all but worthless anyway, so insist that the arresting officer take you in and administer a sobriety test at the precinct. You're within your rights to do so—and, hey, if your blood-alcohol level drops by the time they get around to actually giving you the test, so much the better.

**DO TAKE YOUR TIME CHOOSING A DEFENSE ATTORNEY**—let's say they've got you red-handed, caught you in some act and hauled your ass to jail. There might be some pressure on you to reach for counsel right away, but shop around. How? Ask a court officer for a recommendation. Be up-front about it, say it's your first time in the system and you could use a little guidance. Nine times out of ten, you'll get a helpful response. If you're already "inside," ask another inmate. Then get a second opinion, maybe even a third. You can always switch things up later on, but you want to get this one right straight out of the gate—it'll save you a whole bunch of time *and* a whole lot of heartache. Also, if you're looking to do better than a court-appointed attorney, don't throw in with the first schmuck you see outside the courthouse trolling for business. Have a friend or family member make a couple calls.

**DON'T TALK TO THE POLICE**—you've probably seen enough cop shows to know you're supposed to "lawyer up" when you're in custody, so take a page from those Hollywood scripts. Plead the Fifth, and shut the fuck up, even if the arresting officer is as nice as nice can be. A lot of times, you'll draw the friendly half of a good-cop/bad-cop team, and you'll be encouraged to talk, but keep a lid on it. The more you talk, the more trouble you'll make for yourself, without even realizing it.

**DON'T TALK TO ANYONE ELSE, EITHER**—don't be running your mouth on the inside. Even if you're just in a holding cell, waiting to be processed, you have to assume everyone else in there with you is out to do you dirt. You're not in jail to make friends. Guys may come on all friendly and try to get close, and you might welcome the company because prison can be a pretty lonely place. But you're reaching back out at your own peril because, as often as not, when you share information with another inmate, he knows where you live, where you used to work, the names of your kids . . . he'll find a way to shake you down, use that information against you before long. Maybe he'll get out before you and start making trouble for your family, so you'll be smart to keep your head down and your lips sealed. That said, I know it'll be hard to tune out the other inmates entirely, but don't tell anyone what you're in for. Be as vague as possible. If you feel you have to cop to something to be taken seriously, tell people you're in for assault—that covers a whole lot of nonspecific ground. Whatever you do, if you're in for some type of sexual crime, do not come anywhere close to mentioning it. Last thing you want is to put it out there that you're some type of predator or pervert—a kiss-of-death label you do not want to wear.

**DO MAKE YOUR FIRST PHONE CALL TO A BONDSMAN**—this one might seem self-serving, coming from a bondsman, but let's face it, your lawyer can't get you out. Your bondsman can. Plus, a good bondsman can make all those secondary calls for you. He can set things up with your attorney, with your family, with your place of business. He can run interference. And keep in mind, when they tell you you're entitled to one phone call, it's not *just* one phone call. It's not one and done. Once you're processed and inside, you can always stand in line and use the prison phone, so it makes sense to get your bail working as quickly as possible. Everything else can wait.

**DON'T ACCEPT ANY FOOD OR DRINK WHEN YOU'RE IN CUSTODY**—if you're brought in for questioning, and an officer asks you if you want a Coke or maybe something to eat, politely decline. Why? You'll leave behind a trace of DNA or a set of prints they can run and use against you. Might seem like an excessive, paranoid response to being in a tough spot, but if you're a career criminal—if you're "in the industry," as we like to say—you'll present investigators with a bunch of new and unnecessary ways to screw you. They'll pick something up off a Coke can, a half-eaten sandwich, a discarded wrapper . . . whatever. I've even heard of cases where they took a sample off a guy from a used tissue. So keep your nose clean, keep your hands in your pockets, and get something to eat later.

**DON'T TRUST A PRISON PHONE**—okay, so this piece of advice kind of cuts against a previous piece of advice, but hear me out. Every phone you'll use in prison is tapped. Your conversations are all monitored. Prison officials won't tell you this, and in some cases your lawyer won't even tell you this, but you can count on it. Attorney-client privilege? It doesn't mean shit if you're talking on a prison phone. Privacy between husband and wife? Doesn't mean shit, either. Go ahead and say what needs saying, but be aware that anything you say can and will be used against you.

**DO DRESS TO IMPRESS**—as much as possible, you want to make a good impression. If you've got a court appearance, show the judge respect. Show the jury respect. If you're already in custody, have a friend or family member bring you appropriate clothing, so you don't turn up for your court date in a jumpsuit. Yeah, *orange is the new black*, like it says on that great new Netflix show, but it doesn't exactly buy you a lot of admiring looks away from the yard. You're much better off in a navy-blue suit, if you can arrange for one. And speaking of a show of respect, make sure to maintain eye contact with the judge when he or she is talking to you. Look straight at the jury during the trial. Never put your head down, never shake your head, never slump your shoulders or look defeated. Carry yourself with dignity and confidence. And, if it's appropriate, don't be afraid to smile.

**DO SURRENDER**—that is, if they're mounting a strong case against you. You'll be able to tell, believe me—like, if they execute a search warrant for your home or office, you can pretty much count on getting pinched, so it's smart to cooperate. Make it tough on them and they'll make it tough on you, so take the time to line up a bondsman and get a bail package together so you can get out the door as soon as you step in.

**DON'T LET THEM BRING YOU IN AGAINST YOUR WILL**—a good lawyer will help you dictate the terms of your surrender. You don't want to enter the system wearing cuffs or shackles. Come in on your own terms with your head held high if you can.

**DO PREPARE YOUR SPOUSE AND YOUR FAMILY FOR WHAT'S COMING**—be straight with the people you love. Let them know what to expect— even if you're not quite sure yourself. (Figure it out!) Talk about the frequency of conjugal visits, and how they might go. Talk about full-family visits, and how they might go. Talk about how you'll communicate back and forth between visits. Take as much of the mystery out of prison as you can, going in.

**DO HIRE A PRISON COACH**—that is, if one's available. In and around most major cities, you're able to hire ex-cons or prison "experts" to help coach you and your family over these next paces. Hire the best you can afford—it'll be money well spent. Coaches charge anywhere from $150 to $350 per hour, depending on where you live and their level of expertise, but after just a couple hours you'll be better positioned to navigate your way through the system.

**DON'T LET FRIENDS AND FAMILY BRING IN ANY CONTRABAND**—this one seems like a no-brainer, but you'd be amazed how many people try to smuggle shit in when they go to visit their loved ones inside. I'm not *just* talking about drugs or weapons here. Different prisons have different guidelines, and it's on you to make sure your visitors follow them. Food, magazines, bobby pins, certain items of clothing . . . know what's allowed and what's not.

**DON'T MAKE WAVES**—in other words, lie low. Try not to call attention to yourself on the inside. Blend into the background. Go unnoticed.

**DO PAY ATTENTION TO THE PRISON CULTURE**—figure out the lay of the land right away, either on your own or with the help of a coach or a plugged-in "rabbi." Don't wear the wrong colors if you're not gang-affiliated. (And if you *are* gang-affiliated, this goes without saying.) If you're a "civilian," let it be known that you're not a gangbanger and that you're not looking for trouble.

**DON'T BACK DOWN**—especially if a fight is inevitable. I know I just said it's best to stay out of trouble, but sometimes trouble can't be avoided. Sometimes it finds you. On the inside, the best way to make trouble go away is to beat it into the ground. It's never a good idea to fight inside, but you've got to fight for respect. If you have to, find the toughest, baddest motherfucker and step to him. Even if you get hurt, go. Even if you get jacked up for it later on, go. And when you "go" inside—meaning, when you fight—you *go*! There's no waiting for someone to put a stop to it. There are no referees. You go until you're done. Until you gain respect. It'll put it out there that you're not a punk, that you're not about to take any shit.

**DO KICK YOUR CASE AROUND AS LONG AS YOU CAN**—the system doesn't do you any favors, so don't go doing any favors for the system. If you're out on bail, let your case drag its way to trial. DAs come and go. Headlines come and go. Courts get backed up, overloaded—and if there's one thing judges hate, it's a backlog of cases. Find a way to keep your case on the docket, and you'll get a better deal from the prosecutors.

**DON'T BE A BLOWHARD**—nobody likes a braggart, inside or out. Don't tell your cellmates you're connected to this or that powerful person, even if you are. Don't boast that your father went to school with a particular judge, even if he did. Keep your business to yourself.

**DON'T FUCK YOUR BONDSMAN**—I present this one last, but it's definitely not least, because if you jump on me, if you're less than honest with me, I'll let the world know you can't be trusted and no other bondsman will touch you.

Most of what I tell my clients is just commonsense stuff, but with a lot of the folks I deal with, common sense isn't always a strong suit.

Your best bet: stay the fuck out of trouble—but, just in case, I'm in the yellow pages.

# 7

# Dilemmas

My line of work, the cell phone is like a third arm. Can't imagine how I'd do what I do without it. I'm afraid to miss a piece of business—probably not a healthy approach but it's the only way I know. Satchel Paige had that famous line: "Don't look back. Something might be gaining on you." That's my attitude about work. If I don't pick up the phone, they'll call someone else. Some lawyer will be in a jam, he'll need to spring his client on a moment's notice, he'll call another bondsman, and then he'll have that other bondsman in his Rolodex. No way I'm about to give my competition an edge.

The other bondsmen in town, they'll catch their share of calls, but I won't give them mine.

I've got a crappy little flip phone, battery lasts just about forever. No smartphone. No keypad. My friends give me shit about it. My clients, too. And my kids? To them it looks like something from the Stone Age. It's basic, bare-bones, the kind they give you for free, but it's where my work gets done.

All the time, people call. And I'm there to answer. Even when I'm out to dinner, away on vacation, spending time with my family—I know I should shut off my phone, but I can't. I won't. I've been on the phone in a hot tub in the Bahamas doing bails. I've been at a wedding, a bar mitzvah, doing bails. I've even been to a World Series game at Yankee Stadium, one hand with my phone to my ear, the other wrapped around a hot dog.

Some calls I probably shouldn't take. Like the one that came in not too long ago from a guy I'd bailed out a few years back, another guy who allegedly worked in the "family" business. We'd never discussed his supposed mob ties, except to talk around them. Between the lines, it was understood—one of those better-left-unsaid deals, even though what's left unsaid comes through loud and clear. Since we'd gotten together on a bail, this guy had helped me out, sent a lot of work my way, been a good set of eyes and ears for me, so when I saw his number on my phone, I dropped what I was doing to take his call.

Actually, it wasn't a call. It was a text. That's about the height of my tech-savvy—me and my phone, we're low- to mid-tech, and this guy, he was worse than me. He was old-school, man, so for him to be sending me a text, I figured something was up. He wrote that he needed to speak to me ASAP. The time stamp on the message was 7:14 in the morning, so I took one last sip of my coffee and hit the redial button.

Before I even heard a ring he answered. "Can you meet me this morning, the usual place?"

"Sure. What's up?"

"Better we should meet."

The usual place was a diner in the Bronx, so I grabbed my few things and made for the car—figured, no traffic, I could be there in twenty minutes. Whatever else I had going on that morning, it would have to wait. That's how it goes when there's family business. Everything else goes on the back burner.

I made good time from my house down to the Bronx, but the guy was already in the parking lot when I arrived. He saw me pull up, stepped out of his car, looking like he was about to bust. He had a half-eaten Danish in one hand, a cup of coffee in the other, and a folded-up newspaper jammed in the crook of his right arm. As I approached, he reached for the paper, handed it over. "You see this shit?"

"What?"

"Break-in, Upper West Side? The rape?"

"Yeah, saw that this weekend," I said. "Terrible thing."

I took the paper, but the guy was already telling me the real story, so I leaned against the car and listened. The victim was the daughter of an "associate"—a higher-up in the family business just back from a fourteen-year stretch upstate. A single mother, recently separated. Her attacker was a pizza delivery boy who'd apparently been to the apartment before. Knew the layout. Knew, probably, that this woman was single, that she was an easy mark. Can't imagine the asshole had any idea his victim was mobbed up in just this way.

But that's how it goes, right? You bust through the wrong door, and whatever shit you're in gets a whole lot deeper.

As we were talking, I realized this conversation was the most explicit we've ever had in terms of the family business. The details this guy usually talked around were now completely clear. The pizza delivery asshole, he may or may not have known this woman had a kid, or that the kid was sleeping in the same room when he did the rape, or that the victim's made father had just been released from prison. That part didn't make the papers. The woman's name, it didn't make the papers. Her father's name . . . none of that. But here we were, talking through the whole damn deal, and my go-between was filling in the blanks and turning my stomach.

I didn't want to hear this shit.

How my name came up on this, I've got no idea, but now I was involved, and I didn't like that I was involved. Scared the crap out of me—not because I worried for my safety, but because I didn't like how I looked to myself in the back-and-forth. All along, I was just as ripshit, just as agitated as the guy standing next to me in the parking lot—only now he and his associates were looking to me to do something about it, and for a sickening, long moment I caught myself thinking of ways to do just that.

The father, he wanted to make some kind of next move—some type of eye-for-an-eye retribution. What it was, my guy couldn't say. How it might go down, he couldn't say. All he could say was that this connected father was out for revenge—the kind of revenge that wouldn't go unnoticed, but wouldn't come back to bite the father in the ass, mess with his parole. The kind of revenge you'd expect from a father or a grandfather who'd been shamed, hurt, devastated in just this way.

Next came "the ask"—where I came in.

Bottom line: the go-between wanted to know if I'd give him a name, someone his associates could squeeze on the inside, make it rough for this pizza delivery asshole. The father, he wasn't willing to trust this kid's fate to the criminal justice system—not completely. So they wanted to know what it was like in the Rikers Island adolescent facility, the RNDC. They wanted to understand the culture.

The RNDC population is eighteen and under, and these mob guys, they don't reach into that territory—not exactly their wheelhouse. The way it works, in the adult facilities, you can put your head down and do your time. Rikers is such a shithole, most guys just want to get out of there and head upstate to start their bids. They don't want any trouble. But these young kids, they need to make their bones. Plus, they're warehoused in a dormitory-style setup. Typically, they don't stay one or two to a cell. There's bunk after bunk after bunk, so it doesn't take much to set things off.

What goes on is mostly gang activity. If you're not affiliated, if you're not wearing colors, you're fucked. It's bad on top of bad on top of bad. It's such a crazy, messed-up, pressure-cooker environment, everyone kicking up some dust, it made sense these mob guys might need someone to walk them through it. And it made sense them reaching out to me, because I was wired into the place. I knew all the punks who ran the show there: the Latin Kings, Dominicans Don't Play (DDP), the Bloods, the Crips, the MS-13s . . . they've each got a presence inside. And those are just the big gangs. You've also got the Post-13s, from Thirteenth Street; the Nomads, from Eighty-Sixth Street; a bunch of different local splinter groups. All these kids trying to make a name for themselves, all at the same time, alongside all these gangbangers, trying to carve out their little pieces of turf. Everybody scrambling for protection, looking to line things up so things might go easy— or, at least, as easy as possible.

My go-between wanted to turn the tables, make *me* the go-between, maybe let him and his associates know a little bit more about the culture in these adolescent facilities. But it wasn't just a civics lesson, these guys were after—no, they also wanted me to give up a name. A big-time Crip, a Blood, a DDP . . . someone they could sit down with, maybe set some things in motion.

This guy in the parking lot didn't come right out and ask for anything, but I knew just what he wanted from me. We'd spent so many years talking around and around so much shit his meaning was clear. The implications, too. I give up a name, someone from the family reaches out, next thing you know this asshole pizza delivery guy gets jacked up in unthinkable ways—which, I've got to admit, wouldn't have been the worst thing in the world. Still, it put me fat in the middle of an ethical dilemma, and I don't do too well with ethical dilemmas. On the one hand, my moral compass was telling me this was a no-brainer. I wanted to see this guy hurt, bad. Whatever came his way, he deserved it—only, as an officer of the court (by extension, at least), I couldn't be a part of it. I could only trust our criminal justice system to do the right thing, even knowing full well that what this asshole did to this woman—in front of her son, no less—was unconscionable, reprehensible.

Told myself, Hey, he doesn't deserve to be protected from any of the fallout that comes his way from what he's done. Also told myself, Hey, he's entitled to do his time and move on, so there was this great tug and pull between what I thought was right and what I thought was doable.

I might have wanted to help, but I couldn't. Not really. Not easily.

So, I was torn. Hell yeah, I was torn—ripped apart inside because in addition to being a licensed bail bondsman, in addition to having good and deep contacts throughout the criminal justice system, I'm also a parent. And what this pizza delivery asshole was accused of doing . . . well, it sickened me. I knew enough to know he wasn't about to be rehabilitated on the inside, find a way to turn his life around.

There's no road map for stuff like this. It's not something I could have learned from my uncle Phil or found on my licensing tests. So what did I do? Nothing, for the time being. I got back in my car and continued south to my office in Manhattan, the whole time thinking who the hell I could call. There weren't a whole lot of people I could talk to on this. I couldn't talk to any of the lawyers I worked with, obviously. I couldn't talk to my wife and maybe put her in the same tough spot that I was now in. I could talk to my pal Damon, though. Damon Romanelli, one of my closest friends—a guy who'd seen everything, done everything. I got him on the phone and laid it out for him.

He heard me out and didn't even pause to think it through. "You give up the name, set up the meeting. This animal's gotta die."

Soon as he said this, I knew why I'd called. Damon cut through the bullshit and the chickenshit, both. He wasn't afraid to say what needed to be said—what I was thinking all along.

I took his point, but I couldn't act on it.

Damon understood my dilemma, tried to push me toward his way of thinking: "If I was inside, we wouldn't even be having this conversation."

This was true enough, but it didn't help me. It didn't help me because there was no way to keep this thing from circling back. I could lose my license, my home, my family . . . I could lose everything. Let's say I gave up a name and things started to happen. Let's say it's the name of a King, and he ends up getting his people to rough up the pizza delivery asshole, give him what he deserves. And it won't *just* be a beating, *just* to make a point. No, they'll put this kid in the hospital, leave him just short of his dying breath, and then when the prison docs patch him up and send him back, they'll pound the shit out of him again. And again. This will go on, and on, and on, and folks will look the other way . . . until they won't. Let's say, a couple years down the road, this same King takes a pinch, and he's looking at federal time. It's only natural he thinks to help himself, maybe cut a deal, and says, "How 'bout if I give you something I set up a couple years back?"

Easy to see how this thing can come back to bite me. Easy to see how I give up a name and I'm exposed. These mob guys, I could trust them. There's a code. But these gangbangers, who the hell knows? Still, back of my mind, I'd like to see this kid hurt. I'd like to see him pay.

I busied myself with work, but I couldn't concentrate. I had to appear in court later that afternoon, but I was just going through the motions. A mother came into the office to put together a bail package for her kid, and I was on autopilot. I was shaking. I was all coiled up, unsure what to do, so I reached back out to another made gentleman of my professional acquaintance, from a different branch of the family business, to get his take. All day long, I was dodging calls, texts, from my go-between. He said he'd give me time to think about it, but now he wanted some kind of answer from me. I was afraid to give him one. I wasn't cut like my buddy Damon. Bullshit, chickenshit . . . either way, I was vulnerable.

I thought, If I tell these connected guys, no, I can't hook them up with a name, I risk losing their business, their respect.

I thought, If I do what they ask, I'm screwed in all these other ways.

Best I could hope for was for this thing to go away. My other family contact, he said he'd try to intercede, let it be known that I'm a civilian, that I've got no real skin in this game, maybe get his associates thinking they don't need me to arrange a meet. And they don't, but that doesn't keep them from asking.

Meanwhile, the phone at my side kept vibrating. A private number, over and over. After a while, I shut the thing off—something I *never* do. Like, ever.

Couldn't think what the hell to say if I answered.


My man, Damon.

As long as I'm on him, might as well share another Damon story—not exactly about him, but he was all over it. My eyes and ears on the ground.

This one also turned on an ethical dilemma—not mine, but my client's.

It started when I wrote a $100,000 bond for a Brooklyn rabbi named Baruch Lebovits. According to his lawyer, the rabbi had been charged with sexual abuse and been offered several different types of pleas with no jail time. He refused the pleas, which got me curious enough to do the bail.

The ethical dilemma? What do you do when you're determined to prove your innocence, even in the face of jail time, when the price of your freedom includes copping to a lesser charge? For a man of character like Rabbi Lebovits, you take your chances, do whatever you have to do to set things right. Even if it means doing time.

I never met the rabbi, but dozens of people came to see me on his behalf. Sometimes, it looked like every Orthodox Jew in

Brooklyn was crammed into my office, all dressed out with their fine hats and heavy black garb. They were offering to put up their homes, their businesses . . . whatever it took to free their beloved rabbi. Clearly, the man was a powerful force in the community, and he was determined to clear his name.

Also, a strange twist, but it was a pretty straightforward bond—easy bail package, zero flight risk, no surprises.

About a year later, the case went to trial and the rabbi was convicted—sentenced up to thirty-two years on eight sexual abuse counts. The rabbi's followers were shocked, outraged. News stories told of demonstrations, rallies in support of the rabbi, who many believed had been wrongly accused. I didn't follow the case all that closely, but there was something funny about it—*funny* as in "off." A respected community leader, a father of seven, a grandfather of twenty-four, doesn't turn down a plea deal with no jail time if he's guilty. Yet here he was, facing major years, for despicable crimes he insisted he didn't commit.

At first, Rabbi Lebovits was sent back to Rikers and then on to downstate. The bail was cleared and I went about the rest of my business. Eventually, he was sent to Clinton Correctional Facility in way, way upstate New York, in a little town called Dannemora, not far from the Canadian border. Clinton is an out-of-the-way maximum-security prison. Over the years, it's been home to David Berkowitz, Tupac Shakur, Lucky Luciano, and Robert Chambers, the "preppy killer." It's an interesting place—kind of creepy, I'm told—with its own culture, its own customs. The town of Dannemora was built around the prison, the guards live down the street, so the entire region is all about the facility. It's like the local industry.

I had no idea the rabbi was doing his bid up at Clinton because, like I said, I wasn't following the case, until I got a call from a criminal defense attorney named Arthur Aidala. I'd known Arthur for years, we'd worked together on a bunch of cases, so I was always happy to hear from him. He was a great lawyer, a great friend, and here he was looking at a pretty unusual set of circumstances.

"Ira, this rabbi from Brooklyn," he said. "If I get an appeal bond, would you be able to write it?"

"No problem, Artie. Since when are you on this case?"

"They've switched things up, brought me in."

The appeal was denied, so they never called me in to do the bond, but soon after that they brought in Alan Dershowitz, one of the best appeals guys in the country, and on the strength of Dershowitz's argument the appeal was reopened. Somehow, Dershowitz got the rabbi a bail pending appeal, so Arthur called me up again to see if I could set it up. "The judge has ordered a $250,000 cash bail, with an ankle bracelet."

"A cash bail?" I asked, making sure.

"Yep, you got it."

"Hate to tell you this Artie, but if it's cash, I'm out. I can only do a bond."

The cash deal was complicated for other reasons, beyond just me. For one thing, there was no one upstate to collect and process the money on such a tight timetable. Even if the rabbi could scrape together the cash, his lawyers could never slog through the paperwork hassle and still meet their Passover deadline. My own complication was less complicated: I'm a licensed bail *bondsman*. Cash transactions, that's a whole other deal.

This was troubling to Arthur because he had it in his head that I would do the bail—one less thing for him to worry about, I guess. It was troubling to me, too, because I never liked to be shut out of a potential fee. But Arthur said he wanted me involved, anyway: "We don't even know where the money is supposed to go. There's nobody who'll take it. Figure out a way to make it happen for us and we'll cut you in."

This was a strange case, no question. Normally, you pay the bail through the Department of Corrections. A whole system is in place to process these cash payments, but when you go this route, it can sometimes take as long as three to four weeks. Rabbi Lebovits didn't have three to four weeks, apparently. It was April, and Passover was approaching, and his people wanted him home for the start of the holiday, which was less than a week away. The guy had already been up at Clinton for over a year, had missed the last Passover, so now that he'd been granted this bail pending appeal, the idea of his being home for the holiday was all-important. To him, to his family, to his congregation, it was a big, big deal.

I told Arthur I'd make a couple calls—only each call took me further and further from getting this thing resolved.

I called Arthur back the next day and filled him in—told him Clinton wasn't set up to take the money because the rabbi was a sentenced prisoner. Told him the Supreme Court down in Brooklyn wouldn't take it because they didn't have the rabbi in their system as a custody—meaning, he was outside their jurisdiction. "With a cash bail," I said, "there's no way to get him back to Brooklyn in less than three weeks."

Same thing I'd told him when he first brought it up, but now it's like I was reporting back to him instead of just telling him what I already knew, so it carried a little more weight.

I could hear Arthur sigh, like I'd just given him the worst pos sible news. "Oh, man, Ira. What am I gonna do? I told his people I'd have him home by Passover."

It was a Wednesday afternoon, April 13, 2011. The first night of Passover was the following Monday, April 18—not a whole lot of time to pull off this kind of transfer. The main holdup was the cash bail. I laid it all out for Arthur, explained to him that if we could do it as a bond, I could take the paperwork directly to Clinton and arrange for the rabbi's release.

"Will they accept that?" Arthur asked.

"Don't see why not, but I'm being selfish here. I'm looking to get myself in the deal."

"I don't give a shit if you're being selfish, long as we get the rabbi home. What about the bracelet? Can you do the bracelet?"

I told him I could do the bracelet.

Arthur needed to go back to the judge and ask for a bond alternative—meaning, a bond as an alternative to cash. It was an unusual request, but like I said, this was an unusual case, and we had some good people behind it. Arthur Aidala, Alan Dershowitz, me . . . I had to think the judge would take us seriously on this, just on our reputations alone.

Sure enough, that's just what happened. Arthur went with Alan Dershowitz to the appellate judge, and the rabbi was granted a $500,000 bond over $250,000 in cash, with home confinement and a bracelet—doable, reasonable restrictions, we all thought. And they opened the door for me to come in and do the bond.

Collateral wasn't any kind of problem with this guy. I knew from the first bail that there was a ton of property, no shortage of friends and congregants willing to put up their homes, their businesses, in support of the rabbi, so I wrote the bail the next day—Thursday. I met Alan Dershowitz for the first time, thought he was a great guy, impressive, on top of the whole situation. We got the bond signed, delivered it ourselves to the clerk's office, and waited around while they faxed it up to Clinton, followed by a phone call to make sure all our paperwork was in order. We were pushing hard to get this through in a timely fashion, only we didn't quite make it all the way through by close of business on Thursday, so we had to do some follow-up the next day. All of a sudden, we were facing another deadline, because the court system shuts down over the weekend, so if I we couldn't get this thing set on Friday, there was no way the rabbi would make it all the way back to Brooklyn by sundown Monday.

Wasn't exactly smooth sailing. At first, the Kings County Supreme Court judge Deborah Dowling didn't want to sign off on the bond. We had to have the appellate judge call and walk her through all the irregularities in the case, while I sat with Arthur and Alan in her courtroom. It was a bit of a circus, the way we were jumping through all these hoops, looking for all these loopholes in the system. The whole time, back of our minds, this clock was ticking, getting us closer and closer to sundown on Monday.

In the end, Judge Dowling agreed to sign the bond, but only if the rabbi was released into my custody. This meant I'd have to go to Clinton on Monday. This was a problem.

I turned to Arthur Aidala and said, "Artie, I can't be away from work for a full day. And it's Passover. We've got twenty-five people coming to the house. My wife will string me up."

We worked it out that a representative from my office could stand in for me up in Clinton, so I reached out to Damon, to see if he'd do the honors. Damon turned out to be an interesting choice, because he knew Clinton well. He'd served almost six years there for attempted murder. In a million years, Alan Dershowitz and

Arthur Aidala could never have imagined I'd send an ex-con to represent me on this—an ex-con who'd done his bid at Clinton, no less—but there wasn't a better man for the job, far as I was concerned.

Damon, he wasn't so sure. I laid it out for him, told him how everything would go, and he couldn't believe it. "They're just gonna release him? To *me*?"

"Yeah, long as you've got a picture ID."

Damon explained how people would recognize him, how the guards up there tended to stay put, generation after generation. He'd been out almost ten years, but he knew he'd be spotted— what he didn't know was if this would get in the way of our business with the rabbi, or if it might jack him up in some other way.

"This rabbi, what's he in for?" he asked, almost as an afterthought.

"Sexual molestation."

Dead silence on the other end of the phone. Then, after a couple beats, Damon finally said, "You're fucking kidding me, Ira. You mean, like, with a child?"

To Damon, a child molester was the lowest of the low—he'd rather hang out with a cold-blooded murderer.

"Damon, this is a fucking rabbi we're talking about. I'm telling you, the guy is innocent."

Of course, I knew no such thing—not incontrovertibly—but the two lawyers had shared some of the details of their appeal, enough so I had every reason to believe in this guy. Something about an officer of the rabbi's congregation extorting money and then lashing out at Lebovits when the rabbi called him on it, hiring some teenager to come out and make these outrageous claims. The story seemed to match up with the rabbi's refusal to take a plea.

Damon wasn't buying it, not 100 percent. "When you bailed out Lawrence Taylor, I would have been happy to go and get him for you. Lindsay Lohan, I'd have worn a rubber to go and get *her*. But this guy, a convicted sex offender, a four-hundred-pound Orthodox rabbi, and you're sending me to get him out of Clinton Correctional . . . Ira, I'm not so sure."

"Damon, if you're uncomfortable about this in any way, just say the word."

He thought about it for another couple beats before agreeing to go. He was uncomfortable, but not enough to leave me hanging. He'd do the job.

The four-hundred-pound comment, I should mention, was probably an overstatement on Damon's part—probably a little on the cruel side. Yes, Rabbi Lebovits was a big man, but not *that* big—he was well over three hundred pounds, though, and with his big, gray beard he looked like a disheveled Santa Claus. Damon worried how he'd fit the man in his tiny Prius compact for the long ride back to Brooklyn, but I told him it wouldn't be a problem— the whole time thinking, Actually, this *could* be a problem.

That Sunday, Damon came by my house around midnight to go over the last-minute details. The plan was for him to leave from there. It was about a six-hour drive. The prison offices opened at nine o'clock, so we wanted to leave a cushion. If everything went according to plan, they'd be out the gate in less than an hour, with plenty of time to make it back to Brooklyn before sundown on Monday.

I spoke to Damon on the phone, on and off, the whole way up. I finally drifted off around four or five in the morning, but Blake came to wake me at a quarter to eight. She had Damon on the house phone, and there was a problem with the bond.

I grabbed the phone. "What's up?"

"They won't release him."

"What are you talking about?" I asked, rubbing the sleep out of my eyes.

"They're saying our paperwork's wrong. I drove all this fuckin' way and our paperwork's wrong."

"Our paperwork's not wrong. The woman I've been talking to gets in at nine." I gave him her name. "Just relax, man. Nine o'clock, you go talk to her."

Damon wasn't just frustrated. He was also having a mini-panic-attack—second and third thoughts about returning to Dannemora. He was getting the runaround from all these guards he still somehow recognized. "These fucking animals," he said. "They better not fucking remember me, man."

Nine o'clock, Damon got our situation squared away, and he went back to the guards to present the paperwork. The guards were still giving him a hard time because they'd never seen this type of situation—never seen a prisoner let loose from a maximum-security prison unless he'd been paroled and was leaving in the custody of a bondsman. The whole thing made no sense to them, so they started peppering Damon with questions. Was he carrying a piece? Was he a licensed bounty? They asked for his identification, and one of the guards read his name out loud. The other one picked up on it. "Romanelli? We had a Romanelli here a couple years back. Not a name you see every day."

"No, it's not," Damon said.

"Any relation?"

"Yeah," Damon said, not giving anything away unless he absolutely had to.

"What? Father? Brother? Cousin?"

"Me, actually," Damon said finally.

The guards weren't expecting this, obviously. One of them reached for his gun—a stupid, knee-jerk response, I thought, when Damon told me the story.

The other one turned to Damon and threw a couple more questions at him: "You were in here? For what? How long?"

*Sure as shit . . . armed robbery . . . six years . . .*

Damon told me later it could have gotten really fucking ugly, but the way it shook out it was just ugly. A lot of words, back and forth, a lot of tension, but the paperwork was good. Everything checked out, although for a beat or two it seemed like the rabbi's fingerprints that came in from Albany didn't match the set they had on file, so that was another drag on our situation.

Next, there was a problem with the rabbi's commissary money and his personal effects. A ton of money was in the rabbi's account—thousands, I was told—because he was looking at a long haul, and he had all these supporters back home who were climbing all over each other to see that his bid went easy. I told Damon not to push about the money, we could sort it out later. The personal effects, though . . . the poor guy needed a set of clothes. All he had was his prison gear, and I hated the idea of sending a man of the rabbi's stature out into the world in a fucking jumpsuit, but it was taking way too much time to get him out the door. He and Damon should have been on the road by nine thirty at the latest, and now it was ten thirty, eleven, and they were still looking at a six-hour drive if they made good time.

Finally, Damon got tired of waiting, so they left without the rabbi's clothes. Damon figured, What the fuck does this guy care? He'll be in the car the whole time.

On the way out, the correctional guards who'd "made" Damon on the way in started giving him another hard time—the rabbi, too. They shouted after them, "Some pair, a fuckin' pedophile and a fuckin' criminal."

Damon turned to go after them, but the rabbi grabbed his arm. For the first time all morning, he addressed Damon by name. "Damon, please. Do not start with these men. You do not know what they've done to me."

In the car, the passenger seat thrown all the way back to accommodate the rabbi's large frame, the two men barely spoke for the first hour or so. After a while, the rabbi asked to borrow Damon's cell phone, and while eavesdropping on the rabbi's end of these conversations, Damon finally came around and accepted the possibility that Baruch Lebovits was innocent. He listened as the rabbi called Marty Markowitz, the Brooklyn borough chief. He listened as he called his family. He listened as he tried to put a call through to Mayor Bloomberg, who wasn't available, so the rabbi spoke to someone else in the mayor's office instead.

This guy had some serious juice, Damon was realizing.

The rabbi was on the phone for almost thirty minutes, Damon told me later, and as he spoke he kept playing with his long, gray beard. It had been all folded up in prison, bunched into a kind of net, and now the rabbi was picking at the netting and the rubber bands and letting it unfurl. It was weird to watch, Damon said, but also fascinating. After a while, the rabbi noticed Damon noticing and started to talk.

"You do not understand what they do to you when they think you have touched a child in this terrible way," he said. "They separate you from the rest of the population. They spit in your food, so you cannot eat it. They call you every fuckin' name you can think of."

Damon told me later how strange it was to hear this beloved community leader use such language—a fuckin' rabbi!—especially in such a thick Jewish accent, but the two men started to warm to each other.

Damon worried about the time, so he was blowing past the speed limit—going eighty miles an hour over some stretches, and as they talked, the rabbi took out a little prayer book he carried with him and started davening—at least I think he was davening, but my pal Damon wasn't the most reliable reporter on this score.

Suddenly, they heard a police siren, and Damon saw a cop car approaching in the rear view. "Rabbi, you better pray faster or we're not gettin' home."

Can't imagine what this highway cop must have thought, peering in Damon's window to find this overweight, gray-bearded man stuffed uncomfortably into the passenger seat, wearing prison clothes, an open prayer book in his lap. The cop overreacted—more than a little, apparently—drew his gun, dragged Damon and the rabbi out of the car, sat them down on the side of the road, slapped a pair of cuffs on them. Damon did his best to explain the situation, but there was no explaining it to this guy. What the cop was seeing didn't match up with anything in his experience.

Finally, Damon persuaded the cop to look for the paperwork in the glove compartment, to call up to Clinton, and the cop was able to check out Damon's story. Took about an hour to sort the whole thing out—an hour we didn't think we had to spare. And the cop was still determined to bust Damon's balls: "I can't just let you go, after all that. You were speeding."

He wrote Damon up on a tinted-window charge.

Four thirty or so, Damon called to tell me he was at the Tappan Zee Bridge. Sunset was at about six thirty, so we were cutting it close. I had my bracelet guy, Manny, waiting at the rabbi's house in Park Slope. I had Arthur Aidala calling me every half hour for a progress report because he, of course, had the rabbi's family, his congregants, calling *him* every half hour. It's like the entire Orthodox community in Brooklyn was dialed in to this one-car motorcade, tracking the rabbi's ride down the New York State Thruway, waiting for this special package to be delivered in time for the holiday.

Meanwhile, my own house was filling up with guests for our own seder, and Blake was on me to put down the phone and help out, take part, but I was completely focused on this drama with the rabbi. "Blake," I kept saying, "I can't talk to you until I get this goddamn thing done."

Inside the car, Damon and the rabbi were chill—getting along great, talking about this and that. Outside the car, the rest of us were tense, nervous as hell.

Damon called back a few minutes later to tell me the rabbi had a request—he wanted to make a stop on the way. He wanted to go to his son's house first and get cleaned up, put on his regular clothes. At another time, this would have struck me as a reasonable request, but I didn't think they'd make it. The son's house was only a few blocks from the rabbi's house, but we still had to get them through holiday rush-hour traffic, still had to get the bracelet on . . . there were all these variables.

Still, how do you say no to such a simple request? The man had his dignity after all.

Damon waited while the rabbi's sons and grandsons raced the rabbi downstairs to get him cleaned up. They helped him wash, dress . . . whatever. Fifteen minutes later, Rabbi Lebovits came up the stairs looking like Superman busting out of a phone booth.

The man was completely transformed, Damon said. In place of this disheveled, dirty, beaten-down man in prison clothes, there was this regal presence.

It was something to see, Damon said—but at the same time the rabbi's appearance gave Damon cause for concern. He worried about the big, black, wide-brimmed hat the rabbi now wore on his head. "Rabbi, that fuckin' hat is not gonna fit in my car."

The rabbi laughed. "I'll stick my head out the window."

At about six fifteen, when the rabbi was out of the car and Manny had the bracelet on him, Damon called: "The matzo ball's been delivered."


A couple footnotes to these two stories. As I write this, the bond on the rabbi is still intact. The conviction has been set aside awaiting a new trial, thanks to the great work of Alan Dershowitz and Arthur Aidala, but the rabbi rejected yet another plea deal that would have given him time served—meaning, he could avoid the risk, the expense, the hassle, of a new trial. He refuses to take a deal. He's off house arrest, off the bracelet, but the bond is intact.

Professionally, this bond turned out to be a big deal for me because the rabbi referred a cantor from his community to me who I've got out on a $2 million bail, so if you add that to the $500,000 bond and the initial $100,000 bail on the rabbi, that's $2.6 million flowing from this one case—a lot of gelt, as my born-again Jewish pal Damon would say.

All of it flowing from this one man and a matter of principle.

That asshole who did the rape, with the woman's kid in the same room? He deserved whatever shitstorm came his way on the back of that, but I couldn't be the one to set that shitstorm in motion. Didn't matter what I *believed*. Didn't matter what I *wanted*. Didn't even matter what was right. Only mattered that I keep myself out of it. The fallout, that's what mattered—so I turned tail. I waited for my go-between to stop calling—and, eventually, he did. Don't know if he and his associates ever found a way to get to this kid on the inside. I'm guessing they did, and that's why the go-between stopped calling.

Professionally, it was a big deal that some important people felt they could trust me with sensitive information, while I was still able to walk that very thin line between getting my hands dirty and *getting my hands dirty*.

How I see it, these two stories, they're like the bail bond business in a nutshell. It's a business of risk, and here you have two ways of assessing risk. There's me, leaning one way but not willing to risk everything just to do what I thought was right. And then there's the rabbi, absolutely willing to risk everything just to clear his name. Good for both of us, I guess.

# 8

# Family

Every night I take a different way home. Sometimes I'll take the Hutch. Sometimes I'll take 95. Sometimes I'll crawl along the side streets. I'll overshoot my exit and double back. I'll take the long way around.

It's the nature of my business—a cash business, a lot of the time. There's always money around, and the folks I work with, they know this, so I check the house every night before I go to bed. Three times. I look out the windows. Three times. I've got weapons stored around the house, just in case—in every room just about. I've set it up so that wherever I am, there's a way to protect myself, a way to protect my family.

That's how it is when you do what I do. You have to be prepared. You have to think like a criminal.

My daughter Ava, she *gets* this, in a wise-beyond-her-years way. It hits her hard, the way I'm out there, shaking things up. She's grown up with me being hypervigilant—me thinking like a criminal—it's no wonder she gets to thinking like a victim. Like something bad is about to happen. She always has a lot on her mind—wise beyond her years, yeah, but up against that wisdom there's also a nervousness, an uncertainty.

It kills me to see her this way—but we deal with it.

Even when she was superlittle, Ava worried. These days, her worries have grown bigger, more specific. Mostly, they have to do with my job—mainly, the *fallout* from my job. I take my work home with me, and she soaks it in. She hears me on the phone, talking to drug dealers, gangsters, murderers, mobsters . . . it's no wonder she's spooked. She worries for herself, for her brother and her sister, for her parents, for her friends. She thinks what I do, the people I associate with, will somehow spill over into how we live.

First time I remember Ava being anxious about anything, she was four or five years old. I tried to help her, in my own bull-headed way, but I made things even worse—like, a million times worse. And what happened had nothing to do with my job as a bondsman—nothing directly, anyway. It had to do with the mind-set I carry with me to work each day, the ways I look out at the world, but that's about as far as it went.

Ava and I were running around on a Saturday afternoon, do-ing our father-daughter thing, and we stopped for lunch at a Mc-Donald's in Mamaroneck, not far from our house. Ava ordered a Happy Meal—chicken nuggets, fries, probably a shake. I sat her down, then went back to the counter to pick up our food, keeping my eyes on her the whole time.

When I got back to our table, I was positioned in such a way that my back was to the table behind me, so I didn't notice the person sitting there. Ava did, though. Whatever she saw, she couldn't look away. We were talking, laughing, having a normal time, and all of a sudden she burst into tears—like, uncontrollable tears. Like, out-of-nowhere tears. I followed her gaze and looked over my shoulder to see what had set her off, and at the table behind me was a big biker dude, done up in leather, earrings, tattoos . . . the works. The guy looked the part, like he'd been sent from Central Casting, even had a mess of chains dangling from his hip. I could see right away what had set Ava off. Something about this guy was eerie, creepy. Wasn't just the costume, although that was certainly part of it. There was a darkness behind his eyes. Probably, he would have had to consult a manual to attempt a smile.

Still, I had no reason to think this guy had actually *done* or *said* anything to Ava to get her so worked up, so my instinct was to lean back and smooth over the situation, because Ava was upset. We were causing a bit of a scene, so I said something to the biker, something like "Oh, don't worry about my daughter. It's nothing personal. She cries a lot, gets upset easy."

The biker said something back—all these years later, I can't remember what it was, except that it was harmless, inconsequential. What I do remember, though, was the sound of this guy's voice, high-pitched, almost cartoonlike. It sounded like he was high on meth, but despite his menacing appearance and weird voice he seemed safe enough, and I hoped Ava would calm down now that she'd seen us interact. But there was no calming her down. She kept looking at this guy—staring and staring, crying and crying. I didn't know what to do, so I collected our food and drinks and walked Ava outside to a picnic table area they had out by the parking lot—thinking maybe a change of scenery would distract her from her fears, whatever they were.

I sat her down, then I went back inside to get her some honey mustard for her chicken nuggets—still keeping my eyes on her the entire time. However, I wasn't watching the biker dude, didn't see him collect *his* food and move with it outside to the same picnic area, so I was a little thrown when I got back to our table and saw that he'd kind of followed us, sat himself down at the next table.

It was odd, unsettling—and that's just how it appeared to me. Can't imagine how it must have appeared to Ava, this guy following us outside like that. Naturally, she kicked it up a notch on the crying, so I turned to the biker and tried to smooth things over again. "My man, I don't know what's gotten into my daughter. For whatever reason, she's scared. Maybe it's your earrings, your tattoos, I don't know."

He kind of shrugged, as if to say, *What do you want me to do?*

"Would you mind maybe going back inside? Or maybe we'll go back inside and you can stay out here, if that's better for you. Either way." I wasn't trying to be confrontational—just direct. I didn't want to move a second time just to have this guy follow us, because that would have sent poor Ava through the fucking roof.

But then things turned confrontational. "It's a free country," the guy said in his squeaky, high-pitched voice. "I can sit where I want." His tone was far from cartoonish, though. It was cold, flat, hard.

Wasn't expecting that—but as this guy spoke, I could see he wasn't right, so I knew I had to remove Ava from the scene as quickly as possible without scaring her any more than this guy already had. I grabbed our food and told Ava we'd finish our meal in the car, said we'd be more comfortable there.

As we stood to leave, the biker stood as well, and here I realized I had to change my approach. I'd been avoiding him, but now I got up in his face. "Is there a problem?"

He said the same words back to me: "Is there a problem?"

"My daughter, she cries a lot. She can't help it."

His high-pitched response: "My daughter, she cries a lot. She can't help it." Mimicking me, egging me on.

I noticed I had butterflies in my stomach—not because I was panicked or tense about having to fight this guy. I've never shied from a fight in my life. For a time I worked as a bouncer in a rough-and-tumble Irish pub on North Avenue in New Rochelle called Tammany Hall, a place where me and my buddies made so much trouble the owner figured it made sense to hire us to keep that kind of trouble away. For a Jewish kid from the suburbs, I was good with my hands. I knew how to box, how to take a punch, how to give back twice as good as I got. I didn't have that kind of fear, but this was different because I had my daughter with me. I didn't want her to see me go off on this guy, but I didn't see how we'd remove ourselves from the scene *unless* I went off on this guy. The way I saw it, the one would have to follow from the other.

We started walking toward the car, and the biker followed. I moved slowly, carefully—the whole time thinking, What the hell am I gonna do? I had no idea. I could sense the fear in my little girl, the uncertainty, but she seemed to relax when I took her in my arms or held her hand, so I clutched her tight, tight, tight on the way to the car. I buckled her into her seat, handed her what was left of her Happy Meal, locked the door.

The biker was on my heels—his motorcycle was parked right next to my car, alongside the drive-through lane. His bike was decked out with stickers—skulls, swastikas . . . whatever. A big decal had the letters FTW—"fuck the world"—not the most comforting message to take in at this moment. I noticed the guy's helmet was dangling from the handlebars.

I moved without thinking. Guess you could say I flipped. I reached the bike a couple steps ahead of the biker, grabbed the helmet, and swung around with it—smashed the guy right in the face. Surprised the shit out of him, judging from the way he staggered back, from the look of blind rage and confusion that seemed to wash over him. I surprised the shit out of myself, too—hey, I wasn't expecting to make that kind of move. Wasn't exactly what the situation called for, I'll admit. It just kind of presented itself, just kind of happened, and once it did, I didn't wait for the biker to respond, to recover. I hit him again, this time with my hands— went to work on him right there in the drive-through lane, and as I pounded on this guy, people pulled up in their cars and started to honk their horns. In my rage, I couldn't tell if they were cheering me on, calling for help, or just signaling for us to get out of their way so they could take their spot in line and place their orders, but there was this sudden rain of noise and yelling and beeping horns and confusion.

All the bottled-up rage and panic I felt, for the way he'd menaced my little girl . . . it just came pouring out of me. I wasn't done yet. I walked over to where the motorcycle was leaning against its kickstand, and I rolled it over to the drive-through lane, where the biker lay bleeding. I half-pushed, half-tossed the bike onto him, like I was the fucking Incredible Hulk. Then, long as I was at it, I hit him a couple more times.

People had gotten out of their cars to see what all the noise and fuss was about. People had spilled out of the McDonald's to watch—the employees, too. It was a huge, sick scene, one I wasn't processing. I remember walking calmly back to my car, getting in, and pulling out of the parking lot.

I wasn't so out of it though that I forgot Ava was there. The whole time, I was crazy with the thought of what she was seeing. I tried not to look at her and hoped like hell she wasn't looking at me—even more, that she hadn't seen through the window, through the rearview mirror, what had just gone down. I tried to catch my breath, but my heart was racing. My clothes were torn a little bit. Blood was on my hands. I looked a mess. Ava, she must have noticed, but I tried to talk around it.

"You still hungry, Aves? You want some more chicken nuggets?"
She shook her head no.
"You ready to head home?"
She nodded her head yes.

I figured the best move here was to lie—it would be a good distraction, I thought. So I started going on about how Daddy and the motorcycle man were just playing, wrestling, having a good time. Like I said, I had to assume she'd seen what was going on, just outside the car. I had to assume she was noticing my clothes, the blood, my general mess and unease, so I needed to address it, even in this bullshit way. But she didn't say anything, just sat quietly in her seat, looking out the window.

We didn't get far once I left the parking lot—a couple blocks maybe—before I was pulled over by a cop. A buddy of mine. He walked over to the driver's-side window, saw the blood on my hands. "Ira, was that you back there, in the McDonald's lot?" Asking, not asking.

"Yeah, that was me. Guy had it coming."

My cop buddy thought about this for a long moment, wondering what to do with me on this. Apparently, someone from the McDonald's had called it in. He'd have to file an incident report, he couldn't just look the other way. But he did. "Get the hell out of here. Go. You were never here."

So I sped off, and Ava never mentioned the incident. I told Blake about it, and she was pissed—at me way more than she was pissed at the biker. She hated that I'd lost it like that in front of our daughter, and I hated it, too, but I just snapped. It's no defense, but that's what happened. This guy was in my face, in my daughter's face, and I felt threatened. Ava's panic became mine.

It's no wonder Ava's on edge. She asks about my work all the time. She follows a case on the news, knows I'm talking to the defendant, and gets it in her head that if I don't get him out of jail the bad guy will be mad at me. Worse, he'll know where we live because it's in the newspaper. He'll know her name, where she goes to school.

For the longest time, she made these little leaps in her head. She's got it under control now, but when she was seven, she wouldn't let us leave her with a babysitter. She wouldn't go to the Bronx or to Manhattan because she'd decided in her little-kid head that's where all the bad guys lived. At eight or nine, she wouldn't get on the school bus because she knew I'd written a bail for a bus driver on a hit-and-run. Once, she mustered up the courage to get on the bus, but then she jumped off because she didn't like the look of the driver. Another time, on a vacation to Mexico with three or four other families, she wouldn't let us go out to dinner and leave her with a babysitter. When we did finally manage to get out the door, she texted us constantly:

*When are you coming home?*
*I heard a noise.*
*The babysitter's looking at me funny.*

It got so bad, I started thinking I could do something else, earn a living some other way. But then I thought back to the late start I'd gotten on *this* career. The long slog I'd put in to get the business up and running. I figured, if I had to do a total reboot, jump-start an entirely new career, I'd never get anywhere, so the thing to do was be patient with Ava, maybe find a way to keep my work at some kind of arm's length from my family.

Because, let's face it, I'm a bail bondsman. It's not just what I do for a living—it's who I am. This is how I define myself, how I carry myself, and once Ava got past her fears and anxieties, I enjoyed seeing my work filtered through the eyes of my children. The older two kids especially, they'd listen in, soak up what they could from their front-row seats around the kitchen table.

Whatever's going on with me, they get caught up in it. Like the time I represented a drug dealer named Michael, jacked up for peddling X to New York City club kids. Michael came to me through a lawyer friend of mine, checked in with me for over a year. Struck me as a solid kid. He'd made some mistakes—come on, the kid was a drug dealer, not an altar boy—but he seemed to want to set things right. But then I looked at his card, noticed he hadn't been checking in. Found out he'd taken a plea deal—six years. No big thing, except it put it out there the kid was a snitch.

Bail was $100,000—a lot of money for a case against a small-timer like Michael, but I had to think the DA was pushing back on him, trying to get him to give up some of his drug-dealing friends. That's the way it works, as often as not—even with these designer-type drugs like ecstasy. They use the small fish to catch the bigger fish, all the way up the food chain. Here the kid had put up a house belonging to his fiancée's mother, so it felt to me like we were in good shape, but then he didn't show for a sentencing date. I didn't find out about it for over a month. I was pissed—but I still thought the house had me covered, so I wasn't too worried. If I only had one case, only one open liability, I would have been on it with both fists, but when you've got thousands of cases, thousands of open liabilities, it's just not possible. You need to rely on the alerts built into the system, and technically this kid's skipping a court date didn't even count as a forfeiture until I was notified. That's when the clock starts ticking and I've got thirty days to find my jumper and get his ass back into court. Outside of that, I could be out the full bail—so even though he'd been missing for about a month, I still had a month to find him before it cost me anything but grief.

Soon as I heard about it, I called my lawyer friend, the one who put us together. "What's the deal with your boy Michael?"

"He's in the wind." Meaning, he jumped. Meaning, the lawyer already knew, didn't think to call. I wanted to rip this guy's throat out, but I didn't want to lose him as a source of business.

As I got off the phone with the lawyer, one of the guys in my office, Winston, told me he knew this kid Michael. Told me he went by the name of Mike Jones on the street. Told me the kid had a Twitter account.

"What's a Twitter account?" I had to ask.

(What, you expect a guy with a not-so-smart flip phone to know about things like Twitter?)

Winston showed me his own Twitter account, explained how it worked. I had no idea what he was talking about—could have been hieroglyphics, all I knew—but I got that this kid was kind of hiding in plain sight. I got that he was in contact with his friends, his drug-dealing associates, in this public way—like a virtual game of peekaboo.

Then Winston showed me the Twitter account of "Mike Jones," where my client announced when he'd be at a club, meeting up with a group of friends. I thought, Not exactly an MIT candidate, this one. Putting his next moves out there for all the world to see.

"I'm calling the family," I said.

Naturally, I had a relationship with the parents. The kid had gone back on his word, missed a court date, probably the parents could fill me in on a couple things. "Don't call the family," Winston said. Thinking ahead. "They'll alert him and he'll run."

I knew this, but I was so angry that this kid had jumped on me, this kid I *trusted*, I wasn't thinking clearly. I was seeing red, instead of black and white.

I played it Winston's way and sent my bounties to the club, but later on the kid tweeted that he wasn't going out after all. He was staying home to watch the Heat-Thunder playoff game on television, so once again I let my anger get the better of me and ignored Winston's advice. I wasn't interested in all this cat-and-mouse bullshit. The thrill of the chase, that was never my thing, so I called the kid's stepfather.

"This is Mr. Judelson, Michael's bail bondsman. We got a problem." I told the stepfather the problem.

"Michael jumped his bond? I didn't know that."

"Don't bullshit me."

"No bullshit. Michael told me everything is okay."

"Where is he?" I asked. Not believing a word of it.

"He's right here. Watching television in the next room. You want to talk to him?"

I cupped the mouthpiece on my phone, indicated to Winston that he should call the bounties, send them to the kid's house while I kept him on the phone.

Michael got on. "Mr. Judelson, I'm so sorry."

"Michael, you can't do this."

"I know, Mr. Judelson. Ira. I got scared, is all. Crazy scared. My lawyer fucked me."

He told me how his lawyer pushed him to do this plea deal, left him looking at a bunch of payback inside. Can't say for sure this was how things went down, but this was how it registered for Michael. However it happened, it left Michael with a six-year haul, way longer than he thought he'd be facing. I didn't tell him they would probably have knocked those six years to two and a half. I didn't want to push the wrong button.

I tried to keep this kid talking, give my bounties time to get to his house. "Michael, I'll talk to the judge, see if they'll let you stay out another couple weeks, get your affairs in order." This was important to him, I was learning. He wanted to set things right with his fiancée, maybe put a couple feelers out, do what he could to see his bid went easy. I told him I could help him find an attorney to handle his appeal. He didn't strike me as the brightest kid in the world, but I was afraid if I kept him on the phone too long he'd get that something was up, so I decided to play it this other way, let him know I was working for him, rooting for him, doing what I could to make sure things went okay for him, here on in.

Immediately after I hung up, I called my bounty hunters—these two Haitian guys I'd been using, father and son, one of them former FBI: "Where the fuck are you?"

They were en route.

"Don't go in until I say so," I said. "And cover the exits." Stuff I shouldn't have to tell them.

Five minutes later, I got a text: *Wow, Ira. Call.*

*Wow, Ira. Call.* I thought, What the fuck kind of text is *that*? I thought, This can't be good. And it wasn't. These fucks told me they ran up the stairs before checking in with me, spooked Michael into running, and he was out the door in nothing flat. They told me this in an aw-shucks kind of way, like, *Hey, what can I tell you? Shit happens!*

Oh, man, I was pissed—like, furiously, hopelessly pissed. And the worst of it was I had my son, Casey, with me. He was done with school for the year, bored at home with nothing to do, so I figured we'd do a Take Your Son to Work Day, do a little bonding before he went off to sleepaway camp for the summer. There he was, listening to his father rant and fume on the phone, cursing out these idiot bounties: "You motherfuckers! You let him get away! That's a hundred thousand dollars! You're fuckin' incompetent! It's like Bounty Hunting fucking 101!"

I was halfway through my tirade before I caught myself, remembered Casey was sitting right next to me, so I toned it down, set the phone aside. I put my hand on Casey's shoulder and said, "Sorry about that, Case."

"Don't worry about it, Dad. We'll get him."

I thought, Who's kid is *this*? I worried I was exposing my eight-year-old son to the wrong kind of language, the wrong kind of environment, and he turned it around and tried to calm me down, tell me everything would work out.

What happened was, soon as Michael bolted, the stepfather started breathing heavily. The bounties thought he was having a heart attack. The mother was screaming that she needed to give him his medication—insulin, I think—only she couldn't give it to him because my guys had put her in cuffs.

It was all a big, crazy, noisy mess, and I couldn't think what to make of it.

We finally sorted it all out, got the stepfather his medicine, figured out what was going on. The handcuffs were probably a bit much, a little outside the bounties' authority, but they could make the case that these people had been harboring a fugitive.

(Any excuse to break out the cuffs, maybe use a little excessive force . . . these bounties were all over it.)

A couple hours later, Michael called me from his cell phone—the first call of many calls over the next few days. There were also a bunch of texts, back and forth—fifty, sixty . . . somewhere in there. The kid wanted to duck out on me, but at the same time he kept reaching out, looking for a way back in.

At first, I tried to be nice, to sugarcoat the situation. I told Michael it wasn't too late to turn things around, give himself up, make this bail-jumping charge go away. Then I started going at this kid, hard. I threatened him. He threatened me. I told him I'd have his parents arrested for helping him get away. I told him he was a fuckin' snitch and I'd set it up to have him fuckin' killed inside. I went a little overboard, but I was ripshit. I wanted to scare this kid to where he pissed his pants and turned himself in.

"Why are you doing this to me?" he asked.

I went off. "Why am *I* doing this to *you*? You took my money. You put up your fiancée's house. You gave me your word."

This went on for a couple days. The whole time, Casey and Ava were getting ready to go off to camp—Casey's first time, but his sister was a veteran. Our household was upside down, getting everything ready for the kids to leave. Our routines were all out of whack. The kids were up late, late at night, past midnight. I didn't realize it, but they were watching me, a corner-of-their-eyes deal, texting with this kid. They could see I was pissed, frustrated.

"Dad, you need to get a new phone," Casey said. "It takes you an hour to write a sentence."

I thought, Great, just what I need. A wiseass.

Then his big sister piped in, "The bad guy, Michael, he's probably got an iPhone."

Another wiseass.


Friday night, June 22, I was still nowhere with this kid. I'd brought in another bounty hunter to hedge my bets. I was on and off the phone with Michael, telling him what he wanted to hear, what I wanted him to think. Each time he checked in, I thought of new ways to play it, and so far nothing was working. So far he was no closer to turning himself in than he was the moment he bolted the scene, ditching my bungling bounties.

My kids were leaving for camp the next morning. Plus, my dog was sick—I'd just found out we had to put him down, and I was heartsick. Hadn't told the kids because I didn't want them to carry this sadness to camp—figured we could tell them when they got home in seven weeks. Still, our household was just a mess of emotions, and on top of all that I was out $100,000, down a couple bounties I didn't think I'd be able to trust again.

Also, Ava's anxiety was kicking back in. The more she knew, the more she worried something would happen to me, to her, to *us* . . . and here I started to think she knew way too much about this kid Michael. I was caught between trying to be honest and open with her, same way I'd always been, and trying to keep things just out of reach, protecting her from any details that might ratchet up her worrying. Still, I couldn't lie to her. I could put off telling her about the dog because in my head that wasn't a lie. In my head, that was just giving out information on a need-to-know basis. But if she asked me something, point-blank, I had to give her a straight answer. I didn't know any other way.

I went into her room to say good-night, make sure she had everything she needed for the ride to camp in the morning. "Michael, your jumper. What did he do?" she asked.

"He sold drugs, honey."

"Is he a bad guy? Will he hurt us?"

"He's a bad man, but he can't hurt us. There's no reason for him to hurt us. He's a bad man in a different way than that."

This seemed to satisfy her, at least for the moment, so I left well enough alone, kissed Ava good-night, headed to Casey's room. He was anxious, too—but not like his sister. He was anxious to get going on his first summer of camp. He couldn't wait to hit the ball field, make new friends, check out the scene. But like his sister, he was also worried about this bail jumper—only he was worried for me, for what it might mean for my business. He tried to buck me up: "Don't worry, Dad. We'll catch him."

"You bet we will."

"Why don't you get that old guy on it?" Meaning, a bounty I'd used on another case. (Yeah, yeah . . . I get it. He knows too much, this kid.)

"That old guy, he's not a licensed bounty," I said. "I wasn't supposed to use him that last time, but he did me a favor. It worked out, but I don't think I can reach out to him again. Anyway, I don't think I'll need to. I think we'll be okay."

The kids went off to camp the next morning, and I had to

put my dog down that afternoon. I was a wreck—emotionally, I was all tied up in knots, and this kid Michael was pulling at these knots. He kept texting, calling—said he's coming in, he's not coming in, whatever mood he was in at the time. I was so fried by this point, so fired up, I'd given up on sweet-talking this kid. Now it was all balls and bluster. Now I was sending him texts like *I'm gonna fuckin' chase you down*. Or *I'm gonna fuck with your family*.

My guy Winston was monitoring Michael's Twitter account, and the kid was tweeting things like *A man's gotta do what a man's gotta do*. And *I love my lady, hope to make things right*.

Real cryptic shit, tough to get a read.

Clearly, the guy was all over the place in his thinking, dropping all these clues about his whereabouts, his next move—but I was too emotional to put the clues together.

Meanwhile, too, my bounties were bumping into each other. I heard from one of my Haitian guys, who was upset I'd brought in someone else on the case. "My man, you fucked up," I said. "You had him. I basically gave him to you. I handed you ten thousand dollars, and you fucked up, let him get away."

They were fighting with each other, these bounties, angling for some kind of inside track—but my thing is, whoever gets to this kid first, he's the one entitled to the 10 percent fee. This new-and-improved bounty, the guy I brought in behind the father-son Haitian team, he thought to "ping" Michael's phone, the way the cops do it. He knew a guy at Verizon, set him up with a track-trace, let us pinpoint Michael's location within a mile radius. Every time Michael used his phone—to talk, to tweet, to text—we'd get an idea where he was. The more he used it, the better chance we had of zeroing in on his location.

The following Monday, June 25, I put in a call to Michael's attorney. I was still pissed at this guy, but I needed him to maybe lure Michael in for me, so I gave him a chance to explain himself, maybe set things right. He couldn't help me, though, because the kid had hired a new attorney. The two lawyers were in touch, but my guy was no longer on the case, so I was up against another brick wall.

Summer camps these days, they let the kids keep plugged in to what's going on at home. There's e-mail, phone calls. They post photos online, and we can send photos and old-fashioned letters. It's a regular two-way street. So as the first week or so of camp got under way, I was talking back and forth with Ava and Casey. Each time they reached out—separately, together—they asked after Michael, the jumper. That's what they call him—"the jumper." They didn't ask about their little sister. They didn't ask about the dog. They didn't ask about me or their mother. They wanted to know what was going on with "the jumper."

"Did they catch him?" Casey wrote in an e-mail—no need to clarify the *they* or the *him*.

Ava called, wanted to know the same thing, wanted to know what I was doing, exactly, to bring this guy in. She didn't tell me about camp, about her friends, her activities. She just wanted to know about the jumper. She was a little older than her brother, so I gave her a few more details, told her how we were tracing Michael's phone calls, how I'd put a second bounty hunter on the case.

"It's a lot of money, Dad. Will we be able to go to camp next summer?"

This struck me as sweet—sick, but sweet, that my eleven-year-old daughter knew what was at stake.

"We'll be okay, Ava. Don't sweat it."

She couldn't help but worry, my daughter. She gets it from me, and I was shot through with worry on this one. It wasn't the money as much as the hassle, the insult. I had a lien on the house belonging to the fiancée's mother, with just enough to cover the amount of the bail. The house was worth about $340,000 when I wrote the bail two years earlier, they owed about $180,000 on it, so even with a dip in the market there was a small cushion. But it wasn't just the house, the money. I also had my bounties all pissed at each other, pissed at me. I had my reputation, with the DA, with the judge. I had my kids all wired a little too tight over this.

On July 18, a Wednesday, just two days to go before the clock ran out and I was in full forfeiture, my second-string bounty brought Michael in. The bounty had pinged the mother's phone as well, figured out she'd been wiring money to Michael this whole time. My guy followed her to Western Union, and out of that he got a fix on Michael's activity—got him in his sights and gave chase. Michael almost got away again. He jumped in a cab, tried to pull the driver out of the vehicle and steal the car, but the bounty grabbed Michael before he sped away.

End of story—or just about. We brought Michael into court and I told the judge to throw the fucking book at him, told him this kid was a piece of shit, told him whatever I could think to make things go badly for Michael. A lot of judges, you can't talk to them like this, but this particular judge, I had a good relationship with him. We didn't mince words. "The parents, too," I said. "You should bring charges against the fucking parents."

I was pissed. I wanted this punk drug dealer to pay. I wanted his family to pay, for colluding with him, for dicking us around. Yeah, we were bringing him back under the wire, so it hadn't cost me much, just the 10 percent finder's fee I had to pay the bounty—$10,000 in this case. But it went back to how I can't bend over in this business. Someone fucks with you, you fuck with them back. You give as good as you get—otherwise, these assholes will walk all over you. Word gets around, and you're as good as done.

I softened, though, as they brought Michael into court. I talked to him briefly on the way in. He looked distressed, distraught, almost like he'd been crying. He started pouring his heart out, told me again how his first lawyer sold him out, pushed him to take this lousy deal. Told me again how he was scared, how sorry he was for putting me through all this shit. I knew I was off that $100,000 now—at least I *hoped* I was off the $100,000, because I hadn't filed all the motion paperwork just yet, but experience told me this was how it would go, so I could afford to be a little magnanimous. I could cut this kid some slack, maybe help turn things around for him, so I went to the judge and asked him to go easy:

"On second thought, no need to bury him on these bail-jumping charges."

The next Saturday was visiting day at camp, and the way it's set up, it's like the Running of the Jews. They did an article on it in the *New York Times* a couple summers back, looking at this weird little ritual, all these rich, entitled Jewish parents, forced to wait behind some kind of barrier for the precise moment when they're allowed to enter the campgrounds and race to their rich, entitled kids and shower them with gifts and candy and hugs. It'd be funny, this scene, if it wasn't a little creepy, so Blake and I hung back. Our kids knew we wouldn't be the first parents busting into the camp, and we wouldn't be the last.

Blake peeled off to look for Ava, while I went off to look for

Casey. We also had our parents with us, and my little one. I set Charlie under a tree with her grandparents, so they wouldn't have to trek all over camp. There was a lot of activity, parents seeking out their kids—a lot of genuine emotion to go along with all that trumped-up *show* of emotion. I made for Casey's bunk and saw him coming toward me. Soon as he spotted me, he broke into a run, so I did the same, and I collected him into a great bear hug, squeezed him tight, tight, tight. I'd never been away from my little man for this amount of time, and as I picked him up to kiss him, I realized just how much I'd missed him.

First thing out of his mouth: "What's up with the jumper?"

I set Casey down on the ground and could see the follow-up question in his eyes: *Did they catch him?*

"We got him, Case. We got him."

Just then, Blake and Ava approached, and as I collected Ava in my arms for her hugs and kisses, Casey gave her the news:

"Daddy got him."

# 9

## The Paps

It helps to keep my name in the papers. Good for business. The *Post*, the *Daily News* . . . some weeks, you might catch my name a couple times, usually on a headline-making story with an athlete, a rapper, or a high-profile society type. Rappers, I can usually count on them to make some noise—they're in and out of all kinds of stupid, stupid shit, which puts them in and out of trouble.

Probably my most famous rapper client was Ja Rule, a kid from Hollis, Queens, who was arrested with Lil Wayne in July 2007 on gun and drug charges. They were doing a concert at the Beacon Theatre, and they were picked up after the show when a cop saw one of them smoking weed near a tour bus.

I was called in that night by Ja's manager. She walked me through Ja's situation, put me in touch with his wife, filled me in on their assets, and I went to work. With any luck, we thought we could get him out in just a couple hours, but we had a crazy judge on the bench who wanted to stick it to Ja and his crew with high bails, maybe send some kind of message. Wasn't for me to say whether that kind of thing was effective because it's hard to know what money means to some of these guys, when they're rolling in it. It's all relative, you know. When you have it, it means one thing. When you don't, it means something else.

Ja had money, so it wasn't an issue. He put up his house in New Jersey, which was worth about $2 million. The house was enough to cover Ja, his uncle, and their limo driver, who also got pinched that night, so they had me doing the bails for all three. Ja's bail was set at $250,000, his uncle at $100,000, and the limo driver at $25,000—not a bad haul for me, with my cut, and on top of that I had Lil Wayne's bond to push through, so it was a busy night.

It worked out to the good—Ja and his crew didn't even have to spend a single night in jail, and he was extremely grateful for whatever role I might have played in that, and as he started checking in with me, for the months and months leading to his trial, we developed a friendship. You see, one of the ways the court kept tabs on Ja during this time was to hold his passport, which was like another bond in this case because Ja needed to work, needed to travel. Every time he had an overseas gig or a tour, he'd have to reach out and request his passport, and then the court would reach back out to me to see if I approved. He'd call me and say, "Ira, man. I've got to go to Germany to do a show. You cool with that?"

He was constantly on the road, constantly working. I'm a shameless self promoter, so I sent him a few of my custom GOT

BAIL? T-shirts, and he wore one to the BET Awards that year, got a ton of attention. Put it out there that I was the one to call if you got your ass arrested, so he ran a lot of business my way. Fifty Cent's people started calling me. Fabolous. Fat Joe. Got to where they had me on speed dial, man, and it all flowed from Ja. He wanted to see me do well, but he also wanted to see that his friends were taken care of, so it cut both ways.

Sometimes, he'd call just to bullshit. He was following the case of Plaxico Burress, the New York Giants' wide receiver, who was also a client, also up on gun charges. Lil Wayne, too. I had all these guys out on the same charge, and they were looking over their shoulders at each other, trying to guess how things would fall. How it fell for Ja was a two-year sentence, which he began serving in 2011. On top of that, he also received a twenty-eight-month sentence for tax evasion, to run concurrently with the drug and weapons charge. We write to each other all the time, even talk to each other when we can.

So, yeah, Ja Rule was probably my most famous rapper client, and he's certainly become my closest friend among my rapper clients, but he doesn't come with the best story. That honor goes to DMX, who at one time looked like he could have had a career like Jay Z's, until things went a different way for him. His real name was Earl Simmons, and he grew up in Mount Vernon, New York. He was the second rapper in history to release back-to-back #1 albums in the same year, after Tupac Shakur, so this guy was big, big, big. He had it all, man—started appearing in movies, too.

He came to me in June 2004 through my lawyer pal Don't Worry Murray. The charges against DMX were heavy-duty: criminal possession of a weapon, criminal impersonation, criminal mischief, menacing, driving under the influence, and possession of cocaine. He was picked up on his way to JFK, racing to catch a flight. He put a red siren on his car and got his ass arrested for claiming to be a federal agent—not the best move on his part.

Murray called me in, and we got Earl out the next day. First time I met with him outside the court was in a pizzeria, a couple days later, because he didn't have the money to pay my fee the night I did the bail. He did the meet so we could settle up, get to know each other a little. He came with his wife, Tashera, who I thought was a sweetheart. Earl looked a little out of it. This became clearer when our pizza arrived, burning hot from the oven. I couldn't even touch my slice, let alone put it to my lips, but Earl just picked up a slice and took a bite, like it was no big thing. His lips actually started to sizzle, and he didn't even flinch, and then his wife reached over and dabbed at his mouth with a wet napkin. "Boo, be careful. You'll burn yourself."

I liked that she called him Boo.

Got to say, I liked this kid a lot, wanted to steer him straight. He was smart—full of ideas when he wasn't full of shit.

I was in his face, trying to get him to shake his bad habits, to get off whatever drugs he was on, and he seemed to appreciate the effort. Didn't do much to change his behavior, but I think he liked that someone outside his crew gave enough of a shit to call him on some of this stuff. At the end of every meet, he'd stand up and hug me and tell me I was his dog.

Happily for Earl, he received a conditional discharge on that JFK arrest, but he couldn't keep out of trouble—like, he never paid his parking tickets, always drove with a suspended license, didn't think the laws of society applied to him . . . a typical rapper, I guess. There's a mind-set in that community, leaves some of these guys thinking whatever mess they make, someone from their entourage will clean it up. Their business manager, their lawyer, their bondsman . . . whoever.

I wrote him up a couple more times—once on a $25,000 bail on some motor vehicle violations. Here again, Earl didn't have the money at first to pay my fee, told me he was good for it, so I let it slide. He was supposed to come by and pay me the next day, and then the next day, and then the day after that. I was getting tired of chasing him. "You know what, Earl," I said when he called the third or fourth time to make some sorry-ass excuse for not delivering the money, "just get it to me soon as you can."

He owed me some paperwork, too, so I couldn't let this thing drag on forever, but I believed Earl was a man of good intentions. He always *meant* to come by and pay me, but shit would get in the way—not because he didn't have the money, but because he was easily distracted. "No, man, I'm sorry, Ira," he said. "I'll come by today. Where you at?"

I told him I was at my house. It was a Saturday, and I was leaving later that afternoon for my niece's birthday party at the Build-A-Bear store in the Danbury Mall. He called about noon, so he said he'd be by around one. At one o'clock, he called and said he'd be by around two.

At two thirty, Blake looked at me like I was completely crazy to give up my Saturday waiting around for this guy. "He's not coming, Ira."

"He'll come when he comes."

At three o'clock, I called Earl and told him I was headed out. "Maybe tomorrow."

"Nah, nah, nah, man. I'm on my way. Where you headed?"

I told him I was going to my niece's birthday party at the mall.

"No problem, I'll meet you there," he said.

I never thought he'd actually show—by this point he'd blown me off a dozen times—so I didn't think anything of it when Blake and I sat with our kids in a one-lane traffic jam, lined up at the exit for the approach to the mall, and saw a black SUV come flying down the shoulder, making double time. Never occurred to me it was my boy Earl, but soon as we pulled into the mall parking lot about ten minutes later, I saw the same damn car. And who did I see stepping out of that black SUV but Earl "DMX" Simmons, his wife, Tashera, his kids, and some other dude—his cousin or brother, I never knew for sure.

His suburban posse, man.

Earl called out to me across the lot. "Ira, my man!" Came over, gave me a big hug, gave Blake a big hug . . . there were hugs and kisses all around.

"You came, man," I said. "Can't believe you came." Like it was a big deal—because, hey, it *was* a big deal. It was great he was finally making an effort to pay me, but a part of me thought it was even better that he wanted to meet me at the mall—him with his family, me with mine. Thought that was kind of cool.

"Hell, yeah, I came," he said. "Fuckin' Build-A-Bear, man. My kids love that shit."

Then he leaned in and whispered to me, "Your niece, how old is she?"

I told him.

"I'm gonna go get her something." Then he dashed off into the mall, his entourage in tow.

Blake flashed me a look that said, *What the hell was that?*

I flashed her a look back that said, *Damned if I know.*

This guy, he was like the wind. He breezed in and out and all around and you never knew which way he was blowing.

By the time we got to the birthday party, word was buzzing all through the mall that DMX was in the house. The guy was a huge star back then, so folks were pumped to see him. I don't think there'd ever before been such excitement in the Danbury Mall, but DMX was oblivious to it. Either he was used to it, or he didn't give a shit, or it just didn't register. But he was like the Pied Piper. Everywhere he went in that mall, people started to follow him, so by the time he made his way to the Build-A-Bear store, this huge crowd was tailing him. Someone told me later they had to shut the mall down for a stretch, keep anyone from entering, because folks were spilling off the highway and muscling their way in just to get a picture of this guy.

About a half hour after the party started, he came barreling into Build-A-Bear with a pile of gifts from Toys "R" Us for my niece—and a $2,500 check for me. He made a grand entrance out of it, seemed to love all the attention, although it's not like any of the kids at my niece's birthday party had any idea who the fuck he was. Their parents, though . . . they knew. The people in the mall . . . they knew. All these extra security guards were brought in, and it got a little hectic, a little crazy. Changed the whole tone of my niece's birthday party, I'll say that. Don't think my sister-in-law was too happy about it. Hundreds of shoppers were bunched outside the Build-A-Bear doors, taking pictures through the glass, yelling, waving, trying to get Earl's attention. And Earl—bless him—he was moving about the store, shaking hands with all my niece's little friends, telling all their parents that the birthday girl's uncle Ira was just the shit. "Every rapper in the business, they love this guy," he'd say.

After a while, I knew I had to get him out of there. We were spoiling the party, turning it into something it wasn't meant to be, so I went over to Earl and said, "Hey, man, we should go." Meaning me and him both. Blake hung back with our kids for a bit because they were into making their Build-A-Bears, and I think Earl's daughter hung back with his wife to finish up her bear, but I left with Earl and took a lot of the distraction with us.

It was quite a scene, though. Someday, my niece will look back at pictures and wonder what the hell kind of birthday party her parents threw for her when she was little.

Earl never could get out of his own way. Ended up skipping out on this $25,000 bond, and when he did, his wife, Tashera, was all over me to leave the collateral alone—a house, I think. "Please, Ira," she'd call and say. "Just give him some time. Cut him some slack."

I'd cut him a bunch of slack over the years. I'd considered him a friend—still did, even when he bounced on that bail and left me hanging. Still do. I knew he was in Miami, where he'd just been kicked off a movie set. He was flipping out. I didn't want to be the one to push him all the way over.

My only regret regarding DMX was that he let all his opportunities slip away. I didn't mind that I had to chase him for money because he always paid me eventually. I didn't mind that he turned my little niece's birthday party into a sideshow. No, I minded that he never quite got his hands around the career he wanted, the career that was within his grasp. The career he deserved. This kid, he could have had it all, man. The music was always happening for him, and then the movies started happening for him, and you could see he was about to cross over and become a mainstream star, but it never quite worked out.

All this shit got in the way.


Rappers, athletes, drug dealers, mob guys . . . they all help me catch big chunks of media attention. But for some reason a good, old-fashioned prostitution ring sells even more papers. I've worked a couple high-profile madam cases over the years, and I'm always amazed the way reporters eat this shit up.

Prostitution rings run by suburban Westchester soccer moms—that's the mother lode of media attention. It's like the perfect tabloid storm, and I was swept up by it in a big-time way when I represented a woman named Anna Gristina, who was charged with running a high-priced prostitution ring. Right away, it was a giant story. The papers dressed it up like this woman was running one of the biggest brothels in the city. Started calling her "the soccer madam" because she had kids and looked the part. They also called her "the millionaire madam" because she had money. Said she had a client list that reached into every corner of society.

Bail was set at $2 million—a big number. I'd written bonds for more than twice that amount, but if you can write one or two seven-figure bonds in a year, you're doing okay, so I gave chase—me and every other bondsman in town. I put in a call to Anna Gristina's attorney, Peter Gleason. Got his name out of the paper. I'd never heard of him, which I thought was strange, but then I learned he'd only done a couple criminal cases, wasn't really his thing, so that explained it.

I left a message, never heard back.

Then, a few days later, I got a call from him—no mention that he was returning my call, because he wasn't. He was calling at the recommendation of another lawyer, he said, wanted to know if I'd meet with him to discuss the case. I didn't tell him I'd already called, but I figured he probably knew. A powerful attorney, he must have had a call sheet, someone in his office to log the call. But neither of us said anything—so right away our relationship was on shaky ground. Right away, we were scoping each other out, each trying to guess the other's game.

Didn't take long for me to think Peter Gleason was a little out of his element, a little screwy. First sign something was maybe *off* about this guy was he wanted to put up his own loft in Tribeca as collateral for his client's bail, maybe save her my 6 percent fee. I did the quick math in my head, saw $120,000 go right out the window, but it wasn't *just* about my fee. It was that this guy was working some angle. This wasn't how things usually went, an attorney bailing out his client. Most of the time, the judge will insist that the bond come from a licensed bondsman, will see a request like this as a negative, a red flag, so I wanted to save his client the hassle.

The thing to do was to seek a bail reduction. Two million was off the charts—more of a statement bail than one actually based on the charges. It was understood that the DA was putting the squeeze on this woman, hoping to get the names of some of her clients, see how far her business reached.

Peter Gleason, realizing he might need some help on this, called in another attorney, Gary Greenwald. I'd never worked with Gary before, but I knew his name, so I put in a call to make sure he had no problem, me staying on the case.

He called me right back. "*Bubeleh*, let me tell you what we're gonna do."

Greenwald was this old, no-nonsense Jewish guy, spoke with a thick accent, treated everyone like family—only it was more of a dysfunctional family. He knew who I was, he said. Told me he was looking forward to working with me, only we didn't exactly hit the ground running. Judge wouldn't reduce the bail, so we put our heads together, thought the thing to do was get a writ—meaning, a writ of habeas corpus that would hopefully rule on the court's ability to hold our client under these terms. We argued that a bail of this size was an abuse of the court's discretion, but once again we were denied.

The whole time, Anna Gristina was being held at Rikers, and public sentiment was starting to swing in her favor. It didn't hurt that her husband was home with their two kids—the papers played that up, too. Just like that, people started thinking of her as some kind of wronged figure, a beloved outlaw.

It was a tough case to figure. These two lawyers didn't always agree, and I could never guess what they'd pull next, and after a while I got from the husband, Kelvin, that his wife was starting to think about hiring someone else. She didn't know if she could trust these guys, who were running around town cutting deals with tabloid shows like *Extra* and *Inside Edition*. Gleason was even out there telling reporters he planned to start a website to raise money for Anna's bail, like we were in the Wild, Wild West instead of downtown Manhattan, so once the appeal started snaking its way through the system, she decided to change things up. Said she wanted to move on from what had become a media circus, work with someone she could trust.

For whatever reason, she decided to keep me on. This was

mostly a no-brainer—not because I was any great shakes, but because I didn't cost her anything. Not yet, anyway.

Reporters in town knew I was on the case, knew I'd give them a straight-talking comment, so whenever they called, I said I thought the bail was too high. Said my client wasn't a flight risk. Said she deserved to be home with her family while the case went to trial. Said all the right things.

I knew from experience that if the issue of bail went before the appellate division it would probably be reduced. It was a D, non-violent, one count—meaning a nonviolent, Class D felony with only one count of promoting prostitution. There was no legal basis for that $2 million figure. It was just a headline number, meant to get attention, but it's not like this woman was facing fifty-two counts of this, thirty-five counts of that. It was all neat and tidy, so I reached out to the husband. "Kel, listen. This thing is gonna go Anna's way. You need to get your house in order."

I wanted him to come into the office and put a bail package together, so we'd be good to go when the bail was reduced. I wanted this for me and for them both. For me, because I needed to attach my name to this thing in some kind of binding, concrete way if I expected any kind of payday. For them, because Anna had already been up at Rikers for a too-long stretch and I thought she'd be anxious to get the hell out of there.

I didn't know, but another bail package was in the works, which didn't involve me and somehow still involved Gleason's loft. All I knew was that Kelvin didn't have anything I could take to the judge—no collateral, anyway. All I had was his word and my gut, which might have been good enough for me even if it wasn't quite good enough for the court.

Finally, first week of June, my phone vibrated with the news that bail had been reduced to $250,000—a workable number at long last. I was happy for Anna and Kelvin, even if they went another way with their bail package, because it had been a long, public ordeal. But before I could punch in Kelvin's number and tell him the good news, another call came through: the ADA on the case. He was pissed, a little. His office was coming out of this looking suspect, like they were overreaching, so the guy got me on the phone to vent: "You took a pop at me in the paper, saying bail was too high."

"Didn't mean to call you on it, but it was too high," I shot back. "Way too high. We both know that."

"Ira, we're privy to more information than you. This case is not *just* about prostitution."

"Maybe so, but on paper it is."

I explained how I had nothing against the DA's office, how I had the utmost respect for what they do, how I hated that I'd put him in a bad spot, and on and on. He told me that they had Anna on a wiretap, spilling all kinds of secrets, naming names, giving away the store, so we went back and forth on this for a while, agreed to disagree.

By the end of the call, we'd made our repairs because we knew we'd see each other again.

This all went down on a Friday, late, with the understanding that Anna would be released the following Monday, but the case blew up over the weekend. What usually happens, a bail of this size, a package in place, it's on autopilot. You can predict how things might go. But Anna Gristina had already been at Rikers a couple months, was doing mostly okay, so nobody thought an extra weekend inside would mean all that much. The thing to do, we all figured, was make sure we had our paperwork in order, double-check that all our *t*'s were crossed, *i*'s dotted, do it up right Monday morning. But then, Monday morning came around and I got word Anna was renouncing her own bail package.

I'd never heard of something like this, couldn't believe it—couldn't even understand it. I mean, a relatively young woman, separated from her husband, her children, she'll do whatever she can to get home to her family, to get on with her life, and out of nowhere she stiff-armed the package using Gleason's loft as collateral.

Why the hell would she choose to stay inside? Made no sense, that I could see.

I got a call from the ADA, filling me in, but he didn't know the whole story. Nobody knew the whole story. All the ADA knew was the deal was on, and now it was off. All the husband knew was his wife was about ready to burst. All I knew is I was frantic—mostly because I hate it when I don't know what's going on, when I'm blindsided. I couldn't get Anna's attorney on the phone—didn't even know which attorney to call, because she'd cycled through four or five of them, and each still seemed to be hanging on to some piece of business. This right here was probably the nut of the issue, because at the eleventh hour Anna snapped. Told her husband she couldn't deal with the tug-and-pull, her life being stretched in all these different directions—this one, telling her to sell her life-story rights; this one, shopping a book deal; this one, working an exclusive with one of the tabloids. Got to where the only place she felt safe and whole was behind bars, just out of reach.

Turned out the deal that attached to the loft included a big percentage on all these sideline deals, negotiated by all these different lawyers. So in the end the bond bounced back to me, and I scrambled with the husband to put our package together. He wanted to use his brother-in-law's property because he was underwater on his own house. We'd talked about this, early on, then set it aside. I would have written this bond on a handshake because my gut told me this was a good bail, this woman wasn't going anywhere, but I had to sell it to the court.

Monday turned into Tuesday, Tuesday turned into Wednesday, and this woman was still twiddling her thumbs in jail. You'd think she'd be used to it by now, but it was getting to her. Now there was a clock on her ass. Her latest worry was she'd be deported. She was here on a legit green card from Scotland, been living in the States since she was sixteen. But if you're not a citizen and you take a felony, you'll probably get tossed—doesn't matter if your papers are in order. Meanwhile, she had nothing to do up at Rikers but think through all these doomsday scenarios.

It's not so easy, signing on to a case this late in the game. The brother-in-law wouldn't return my phone calls. He was spooked by all the media attention. Kelvin couldn't reach him, either. Finally, the guy called me back Thursday afternoon. He'd looked at the paperwork, had a couple concerns. For one thing, he didn't like that the boilerplate language was so ironclad, the way it tied up his property. I explained it, best I could: "Look, your sister-in-law, she's not my typical client. Most of the people I work with, they're out to screw me. I deal with the Latin Kings. I deal with the Bloods, the Crips, Dominicans Don't Play. Bad guys, trying to beat me, trying to beat the system. The property they put up, the collateral, I look at it hard. That's why the paperwork is ironclad, like you said."

"What if I want to sell the property?"

"So, you'll sell the property. We'll work something out."

"What if I need the house, some other reason? Like maybe I need to take a home equity loan?"

"You call me," I said. "We'll work it out."

Whatever he threw at me, I threw it right back, tried to let him know it wouldn't be a problem. I didn't know this guy beyond his name in my client's folder, but I knew my client. Yeah, I know I wrote earlier that I mostly stay away from cases involving noncitizens because it's easier for them to run on me, but I didn't think Anna was going anywhere. I knew she was probably guilty, but it's not my job to worry about that. It's not even relevant, far as I'm concerned.

The thing about this brother-in-law, he didn't like to be pushed. Said he was feeling backed into a corner. Said he needed some time to think about it.

I heard this and thought, Anna's screwed.

Friday morning, the husband called to tell me his brother-in-law was out.

"Kel," I said, "this guy was looking for a way not to do this deal."

"Tell me what to do, Ira. All these lawyers, all these advisers. Everyone wants something. You're the only one who seems to want to do right by Anna."

This was nice to hear, but it was only partly true. There was something in this for me, too. Publicity—and not just get-your-name-in-papers publicity, but *good* publicity. It was a nonviolent case. This woman didn't kill anybody. She didn't rob a bank or shoot up a liquor store. What she was accused of was not even illegal in some parts of the country, so in terms of getting my name out there, this case was a windfall. Reporters knew I was working the case. They knew I could deliver a decent quote, some good background off the record—so, absolutely, I was working my own angles. It's just that my angles didn't take anything away from this guy's wife, from doing right by her.

Speaking of angles, I even picked up Anna's cellmate, Louise Neathway, as a client—and she was no slouch in the spotlight, either. She was the "other" woman in a complicated case involving New York Yankees general manager Brian Cashman. She'd been charged with extortion and harassment. She'd allegedly had an affair with Cashman, and now she was apparently stalking him, shaking him down—for $6,000. The papers kept referring to her as Cashman's mistress, but that was an overstatement. That the two women were cellmates at Rikers wasn't so unusual, so unlikely, I guess. Why? Because there's only one female prison at Rikers—Rose M. Singer Center, or RMSC—and since both women were caught in high-profile cases, it was almost inevitable they would be thrown together.

The few times I had Anna Gristina on the phone, she'd put Louise on for a couple minutes: "Just say hello to Louise for me, Ira." Trying to help out her roommate, her bondsman, all at once.

Back to the soccer madam: I pushed Anna's husband to find another piece of property I could take as collateral, reminding him again that it couldn't come directly from any joint assets he might have held with his wife. Reminding him the court doesn't let you walk on the back of ill-gotten gains. He mentioned Anna's sister, so we got her on the phone. She wanted to help, but she didn't know that she could. She came across as a strong woman, spoke with a thick Scottish accent. She knew how the system worked—said, "I own my apartment but I can't put it up."

"Why is that?" I asked.

"DA thinks I'm involved. Thinks my money is Anna's money."

I asked if she had any friends, anyone who might put up $50,000. "Get me to fifty and I'll put up the rest, make the friend sign a personal note for the difference."

The sister wasn't sure she heard me right. "That's all you need? Fifty thousand?" Making sure.

"I'll make it work."

"But you're taking a big risk."

I told her it wasn't such a big risk. Told her I didn't think her sister was going anywhere. Told her it was a good bail, long as we got the package approved.

Three hours later, she called me back with the name of her friend. Said the woman had assets over $4 million. Said she'd come into my office, sign the necessary papers. Turned out the friend wasn't so rich, wasn't so willing. She came in, this woman, brought the $50,000, but wouldn't sign for the rest. Said it was the first she was hearing of this, signing for the balance, so I walked her through how I'd laid it out for the sister.

Then I got the sister on the phone. "I thought we were all set."

"You told me all you need is fifty," she said.

"Yeah, fifty in hand. The other two hundred on paper, in a note. I'll put it up myself, for now, but I need the note. Like we talked about."

We went around and around on this, got nowhere.

Soon as I was off the phone with the sister, the friend opened up to me. She was still in my office, wanting to help, telling me how she'd known Anna for twenty, thirty years. How she'd do anything for her and her sister, but she just couldn't sign for two-fifty. She started to cry.

"Don't cry, I'll take care of it," I said.

"How will you take care of it?"

"Just give me the fifty. I'll handle the rest."

"No, I can meet you in the middle."

In the end, she gave me fifty and signed for fifty—not exactly in the middle, but it was the same neighborhood.

Next, I got the ADA on the phone, told him I'd put a bail package together. Told it to him straight—how the friend came in with the first fifty and signed for another fifty, how her financials showed over $4 million in assets, how I was putting up the rest.

"If she jumps, I'm out a buck and a half," I said.

"And you're doing this . . . why?"

I told him why. I told him how this woman wasn't about to jump, how I'd still collect my full fee, how it put me in the spotlight for the next while, kept my name out there. It was like a giant, public game of poker, only the stakes didn't exactly make sense for me. Not in dollars and cents. I was putting $150,000 in the pot to win back $15,000—my 6 percent fee, on the $250,000 bond. In Vegas, those are lousy pot odds, but we weren't in Vegas. Here, I liked my chances.

Finally, at four thirty on a Monday afternoon, a full week after Anna renounced the first bail package, the ADA agreed to the deal. If I'd had any doubts about this ADA, his decision here told me he was one of the good guys, willing to do the right thing. The one stipulation was that Anna needed to wear a monitoring bracelet, so I could track her comings and goings. Typically, in state jurisdiction, you don't need a bracelet. They leave it to the bondsman to track his own client because we're the ones responsible for returning them to court for trial. Bracelets are more of a federal deal. But more and more you're seeing judges at the state level looking for assurances that bondsmen can control and monitor our high-priced clients. It allows us to bring some of these exorbitant bails down to lower, more manageable numbers.

Anyway, we worked it out so Anna was brought down from Rikers in a Department of Corrections vehicle to the detention complex in lower Manhattan known as the Tombs, where we'd be met by my bracelet guy, Manny. We'd sign a bunch of papers and Anna would be released into my custody—that was the drill.

Soon as I saw Anna, she burst into tears. Even though we'd only spoken on the phone, she hugged me like she'd known me forever. She hugged the bracelet guy, too.

"Tell me this is real," she said.

"This is real, Anna," I said. "This is happening."

She had a bunch of questions about the bracelet. All this time, she thought she was being placed under house arrest, but with the bracelet she was free to move around, long as she checked in with me regularly.

How these monitoring bracelets work is pretty interesting. For one thing, they're expensive—about $18 a day, which can run into a lot of money since most cases drag on six months to a year before they get to trial. The client pays for it, on top of my fee, out of pocket—meaning, they can't fold the expense into the overall bond. I try to prepare my clients, help them get their head around the right number, but they see that it's just $18 a day and shrug it off.

Still, for a lot of folks, it's money well spent because the devices allow them to move about freely—according to the terms of the bail package. It means they don't have to check in with me so often. In some cases, they've got no choice. It's the only way the DA will sign off on a release because the court needs some way to monitor a defendant's comings and goings. The tracking is done through a GPS-type device installed in each bracelet, which is placed on the wrist or the ankle of the defendant. It can't be removed except by the monitoring company. I use a company based in Utah called Secure Alert, and every three to five seconds the bracelet sends a signal to the home base, which reroutes the signal to me. If I want to, I can check on the whereabouts of my clients every three to five seconds—but of course I don't want to.

Before we slap one of these things on, we program in all the inclusion zones, according to the bail agreement. After that, if a client steps beyond a designated boundary, I'll get an alert. It takes about ten seconds for the alert signal to travel all the way out to Utah, and then another ten seconds to bounce back to me—wherever I happen to be. The client doesn't get zapped or stunned, like a lot of folks think. It's not like one of those dog collars you place around Fido's neck when you install an invisible fence. It's all very civilized, very high-tech—and the upshot for people like Anna Gristina is they get to mostly move about on their own terms, do their own thing.

I walked her through how it worked, what was expected of her.

"You mean I can go to the gym?" she asked.

"You can go to the gym."

"I can walk my dogs?"

"You can walk your dogs. Just don't walk 'em near the Canadian border."

# 10

# Paying for College

As much as I loved all the press attention that came my way on the back of this or that case, at times I should probably have kept my mouth shut around reporters. Trouble is, I'm not exactly wired this way—goes against every cell in my body—but my big mouth nearly came back to bite me in the ass on the biggest bond I ever wrote.

It's tough to say any one client *made* your career, especially when you've been at it a long while, but the bail I wrote for the former managing director of the International Monetary Fund (IMF) Dominique Strauss-Kahn was a game-changer. The money was eye-popping, jaw-dropping—$5 million. No one had ever written a $5 million bail before—not in New York, not in any other state in the country. No one, that is, but yours truly, because

I'd written another $5 million bond back in 2006, for a stockbroker named Chris Janish, charged with falsely inflating prices in a penny-stock scam. There'd been federal bonds approaching $10 million, but on those the defendant doesn't have to pay a fee, and there's little to no property involved, just personal signatures, so they fall into a whole other category.

But this bail I wrote for Dominique Strauss-Kahn—or DSK, as the New York City tabloids started referring to him once the case broke—wasn't *just* about the money. It was a wild ride all around. It started with a call from Ben Brafman's office—only it wasn't Ben himself. It was May 14, 2011, a Saturday, and Ben's a pretty observant Jew, doesn't work on the Sabbath, so it was one of his associates—Andrea Zellan. "Ira, we're gonna need you tomorrow."

"No problem. What's up?"

Andrea explained that the head of the IMF had been arrested, pulled off a plane, was being held at SVU—the Special Victims Unit, in Harlem. "This is big, Ira. It'll be all over the news. We need you ready."

I got from Andrea that this case was a big deal, but I couldn't understand why. I'd never heard of the IMF. If I had to guess, I would have thought it was a bowling league, but Ben Brafman's office wasn't getting all hot about some bowling league official, I knew that much. I put in a call to my hedge-fund pal Danny Moses. "Danny, what's the IMF?"

"The International Monetary Fund, why?"

I told him why—what little I knew, anyway.

"Dominique Strauss-Kahn?"

"That's the guy," I said. "Just got pulled off a plane."

"What for?"

"Fuck if I know what for."

The news the next day had it everywhere. Dominique Strauss-Kahn had been arrested on charges of sexual assault and attempted rape, after a chambermaid at a midtown hotel came forward claiming he'd forced her to have sex with him. DSK was a leading candidate for the French presidency, so his being met by police and taken from his Paris-bound plane on the tarmac at JFK to face such sensational charges was a big, big story.

By two o'clock in the morning, news of DSK's arrest was all over the place—and by six, my phone was blowing up like crazy. First call I took was from Ben Brafman, who was back on the case. "Sorry to wake you," he said.

I shot back with that old Groucho Marx line: "It's okay, I had to get up anyway to answer the phone."

But Ben wasn't in the mood for jokes—not for *my* jokes, anyway—so I kept my mouth shut as he filled me in. My marching orders were to sit tight, to wait for Ben's next call with instructions on how to proceed, but my phone wouldn't stop vibrating that whole morning. The *Post*, the *Daily News*, 1010 WINS . . . I'd glance at the number on the display screen and let it go to voice mail. I didn't have anything to say to these reporters, wasn't authorized to say anything even if I *had* any information, but mostly I wanted to leave the line open for Ben or someone from his office.

It was a Sunday morning, which meant Blake and I had to run around to a bunch of different sporting events and activities with our kids, so for a while I went about my usual weekend business. But I was going through the motions, just. It was tough to concentrate on my family when I had to keep checking my phone every few minutes, to make sure Ben Brafman wasn't calling.

Finally, around noon, he called with an update. Something

about how the case was dragging, how his biggest concern at this point was getting his client released from custody as soon as possible.

I offered to help on this. "You want me to push this guy through the system?"

"You can do that?" he asked. Curious.

"I know someone in Arraignments."

"See what you can do."

So I did. Thought it made sense to head toward the city, where I'd be in a better position to move things along if the bail came my way, so I worked the phone as I drove. Ben called back a short time later, to tell me we were looking at about a $250,000 bond, maybe $500,000—said to be prepared for a big number. Turned out his numbers were the underestimate of the year, but I didn't know that just yet. All I knew was that traffic was a bitch, but somehow I snaked and turned my way into Manhattan. I was deep into whatever-it-takes mode, and as I pulled up to the courthouse, I saw this pileup of news trucks and media types. I'd never seen so many reporters, so much activity—even after doing bails for Lil Wayne, Ja Rule, Lawrence Taylor, Plaxico Burress, and a long, long list of celebrities. Put all those high-profile cases together, they still wouldn't have gotten close to this.

People pushing up against each other behind police barricades.

Reporters shouting out questions.

Cameras flashing.

It was like the street version of the red carpet on Oscar night—on steroids.

I struggled my way into the courthouse and sought out Ben, learned there'd been a change in strategy. His latest plan was to reserve his bail argument because the DA was asking for *remand*—

meaning, the prosecutor would try to send the case back to a lower court, where the scope of the charges against DSK was bound to change, which would likely mean a higher bail. Ben said there was no sense presenting a bail argument until he knew what his client was facing, until the DA's office showed its hand.

He apologized for asking me to come all the way into the city on a weekend, just to turn me right back around, but I told him not to worry about it. Ben Brafman had been so good to me over the years, my thing with him was to do whatever he asked, no question. Whatever he needed from me, I'd find a way to deliver—no apologies or explanations necessary.

On my way out, I was flagged by a *New York Times* reporter, caught off guard. Like an idiot, I answered a couple questions. I knew a little too much for my own good, and I guess I was just bursting with it. Plus, just in case I haven't already made this clear, I'm a media ham at heart, so if you stick a microphone in my face, my inclination is to talk, because nine times out of ten it's good for my business. It keeps me out in front, in the public eye. But this was that one time in ten when I should have kept my mouth shut.

Ben called me the next morning, after reading the paper. "Ira, I didn't want it out there that the DA was planning to seek a high bail."

"Ben, I'm really sorry."

"Don't worry about it. Just know for next time."

Meanwhile, Ben was preparing to leave the country—on a long-planned trip to Israel—so he was handing off DSK to his associates and planning to monitor the case from overseas.

Meanwhile, too, DSK's wife—Anne Sinclair, a famous broadcast journalist, the French Barbara Walters—was flying to New

York, prepared to meet a cash bail. Before he left on his trip, Ben let me know they were now expecting bail to run as high as $1 million, and that the wife would be able to cover that kind of number. He said she'd already wired money to his office. He wasn't clear on the amount, but thought it might even be as much as $2 million.

I took this to mean there'd be no room in this bond for me and worried I had somehow aced myself out of the deal by talking to the *Times*, but Ben assured me this wasn't the case. "You're my guy, Ira. But if she's got the cash to cover it, if that's acceptable to the court, that's probably how it will go."

A couple days later, I was no closer to this bond than I'd been that Sunday night at the courthouse, but I was still working it like I was on board. A thing like this, you get close to it, close enough to taste, you don't back away easy. I was on and off the phone with my insurance company, telling them to be prepared for a big bond, telling them this was a slam-dunk case. I mean, this was the head of the IMF. He was no kind of flight risk. He couldn't make a move without a flashbulb going off, without the financial markets knowing, so I was ready to write this sucker up to any amount.

Trouble was, I couldn't get a fix on what that amount might be, or if there was even a way for me to carve out a piece, so I started asking around. Nobody knew anything, but a lot of folks seemed to *think* they knew what was going on—a dangerous combination if you're looking for guidance. I even reached out to the Honorable Michael J. Obus, the administrative judge who was hearing the case, to pump him for information. I'd known Judge Obus for years, knew him to be a real voice of reason in the courthouse. A good guy, a funny guy, a bright guy. We had what I would have called a good working relationship, so I found a way to wander by his courtroom one afternoon.

"Good to see you, Your Honor," I said. "I hear you might be getting a writ soon on this DSK case." Meaning, again, a writ of habeas corpus, seeking to move the case from the criminal part to the Supreme Court—meaning, again, a higher bail. Already, I learned, the defense attorneys had floated a $1 million bail package, which had been rejected by the court, so there was no telling how high this thing might go.

"Ira, you know more about what's going on in this building than half the people who work here."

We laughed, then I slipped into the familiar routine I'd been pulling with judges since the night my daughter Ava was born. "Just gotta feed my kids, Your Honor." Working that line again—like this was all the justification I needed, me being a bail bondsman with my hands out, trying to take care of my family.

Judge Obus had heard this from me before, of course. "You're always feeding your kids, Ira."

We shared another laugh, only this time I thought I'd change the subject. "How are your Yankees doing?"

"Ira, don't insult me. You don't want to talk about the Yankees." Laughing still.

This was true enough, so we exchanged another couple pleasantries and I left him to his work—still with no idea where this bail was headed other than up, up, up. I'd confirmed that Anne Sinclair had $2 million in cash, ready to go, so I felt sure I was out of the deal. Maybe I could cut myself in on the ankle bracelet, but that would be it. Word in the courthouse was that the bail would be higher than anyone had speculated, but I couldn't imagine the set of circumstances that would push it from that talked-about

$1 million level all the way past the $2 million Mr. and Mrs. DSK had in hand.

No way it would double, I told myself.

First I was in, then I was out; then I was in, then back out again. By Thursday of that week, I was starting to think this one had slipped away, but then it bounced back to me all over again. I started getting another flurry of calls from reporters, wanting to know if I was back on the case, because it was announced that bail had been set—a $5 million bond, over $1 million in cash.

I immediately called the clerk of the court, Isabelle, to confirm the number. She said she knew I'd be one of her first calls. "You don't disappoint, Ira."

"Spell it out for me, Isabelle."

"A five-million-dollar bond and one million cash."

"Isabelle, are you sure you got that right?"

"Ira, I've been doing this a long time. I've got it right."

It wasn't a $5 million bond *over* $1 million in cash, as first reported. It was a $5 million bond *and* $1 million in cash. The difference was everything. Usually, when a judge sets bail, you'll see a bond and a cash alternative; it's an either-or scenario. But here it was specifically designated as a bond *and* cash—altogether, a $6 million bail package. It meant there'd be a big bond to sit on top of the wife's cash.

Isabelle knew what a distinction like this could mean to a guy like me. "You gonna be involved?"

"Sure hope so."

But it was starting to look like I was getting ahead of myself on this. No one called from Ben Brafman's office. No one called from the office of William Taylor, another lawyer who was acting with Brafman as kind of cocounsel on the case. I could only get in my car and drive home in frustration, so I headed back to Westchester. But as soon as I crossed the Whitestone Bridge and paid the toll, my phone went off—Andrea Zellan again, this time telling me to get my ass back down to Mr. Taylor's office. Naturally, I doubled back, paid the toll again, and broke a couple dozen traffic laws on my way down to Manhattan, the whole way thinking I needed to get there before this deal slipped away from me again.

*Elusive* . . . that's the best word I can think of to describe this bond. Elusive as hell.

First time I met DSK's wife was in Taylor's office that afternoon. For some reason, she was traveling with two navy SEALs who were acting as bodyguards. This was just a couple weeks after the death of Osama bin Laden, so I took the opportunity to push their buttons on this, only these guys were completely stonefaced. They were like the guards at Buckingham Palace, almost like statues. Couldn't get a rise out of either of them, but as I tried to joke with them, I was also trying to listen to the conversations in the rest of Taylor's office, as everyone was scrambling to get a bail package together. This made for an odd few minutes, inside my head, as a bunch of bad bin Laden jokes jockeyed for position alongside all these dollar signs.

The office was pretty much a madhouse, but Anne Sinclair was a regal presence—elegant, beautiful, sophisticated. She was unflappable, especially when you stopped to think about what she was facing, about the charges against her husband. I was trying to eavesdrop without looking like I was eavesdropping, and I saw clearly I would have to slash my fee substantially to get myself cut in on this bond. Already, Anne Sinclair had had $2 million wired over, and there was talk of arranging another $3 million transfer, so I ran some numbers in my head, figured on a bond of this size

I could slash the crap out of my fee and still make a hefty chunk. Like I said, it was a slam-dunk bond, so there wasn't a whole lot to worry about in terms of exposure.

Eventually, William Taylor brought me into the conversation, and we got on the phone with my insurance company to bang out a deal. I told him I could take a couple points off my fee—at this level, that meant a reduction of as much as $120,000. The wife was putting up a house in Washington as collateral, so the insurance company was satisfied, and in the end I wrote the bond for the full $6 million—against the house and $3 million in cash.

When it finally looked like our deal was about to get done, I had a brief exchange with Anne Sinclair. Throughout this entire ordeal, she impressed me as a class act, but I guess she caught me looking at her funny, in a sidelong way. Maybe she was self-conscious. Or maybe she knew that her extra efforts in support of her husband were bound to raise some eyebrows, considering the allegations against him.

She turned to me. "You're probably wondering why I'm doing all of this for him?" Not really asking. She spoke with a French accent, made it sound like whatever she was saying was some sort of gentle secret.

"It's not really my business," I said.

"But it is, in a way, so you should know. I believe in this man. Sometimes, with people, you must believe in them, no matter what you are hearing."

I'd picked up enough in the back-and-forth in the lawyer's office to know something was not right about this case. Everybody in the press had this guy guilty, but to the folks on the inside it seemed that he'd been set up. Maybe someone wanted to do DSK dirt, discredit him in some way, or maybe the chambermaid saw a way to extort money from a wealthy man backed by an important organization. Whatever happened, I did not believe Dominique Strauss-Kahn assaulted this chambermaid. He might have been guilty of infidelity, but something else was going on here, I felt sure. Still, it was not for me to read too much into the case. It was not for me to give a shit whether he ejaculated on the maid's uniform, which was one of the hot-button angles to the story that first week. No, it was only for me to see that he made bail.

And, soon enough, he did.

Dominique Strauss-Kahn was placed under house arrest, but the case against him began to unravel. He was forced to resign his position with the IMF, and he continued to be tried in the tabloids, but behind the scenes there was less and less they could pin on this guy. The more the chambermaid was questioned, the more her credibility was thrown into doubt. Eventually, prosecutors went from thinking they had an open-and-shut case against him to thinking they had built a case almost entirely on the testimony of someone with some serious credibility issues. DSK's lawyers hired a private investigator to look into the chambermaid's past, and they were able to poke all kinds of holes in her story, to where prosecutors ultimately dropped the case.

Just like that, we were done.

For a few long days, it appeared the quick dismissal in this case might cost me because I'd invested in a CD the $3 million cash I'd taken as collateral, in such a way that the interest could flow to me. I'd cleared the whole setup with the attorneys and with my insurance company. The idea was to offset the two points I'd given back to DSK in my fee, and it would have worked out to the good if the case had run a more predictable course. With the case tossed so swiftly, I faced substantial penalties in closing out the CD to exonerate the bond. But the DSK camp stepped up and covered those penalties to make me whole—which was great of them. Unexpected, but great.

Months later, a free man, DSK admitted in a television interview that he did have an "inappropriate" sexual encounter with this chambermaid. He said it was a moral failing on his part, but he insisted that the encounter was consensual, and that it was in no way violent or aggressive. It also came out that he'd had numerous extramarital affairs, and there were reports of orgies and sex trafficking and prostitution rings—all of which helped to keep this case (and my name) in the papers.

For me, the truly "sensational" piece of this story was that I was involved in it at all—and that it was my second $5 million bond in five years. Me, a guy who filed for bankruptcy as a kid, who lived with his parents until he was thirty years old, who didn't get his shit together on a career until he'd tried and failed at a dozen others. Me, a lousy student who barely made it out of college, who briefly held the Get out of Jail Free card for the head of the IMF, while the world financial markets watched and waited to see what happened to this guy.

# 11

# Joey Cupcake

Some of my business is personal. Some of it is just business. Some of it is both—a mash-up, coming at me from all sides. Like how it was with my pal Joseph Urgitano.

For a long time, I didn't even know Joey's last name, just knew him as Joey Cupcake, his name on the street. I met him through my buddy Damon. They did time together, became close—how it goes for a lot of guys I know. You serve time with someone, you make it through, it's like you're joined at the hip. There's no shaking it—like serving together in the military.

(Okay, so there's a difference—like, when you're in the military, you're not in for breaking the law. Like, in the military, you don't have to be ashamed or hide that you're even there. But ask anyone who served, inside *and* out, and they'll tell you the bond is the same.)

Joey was a prison legend. He did twenty years—with strength, dignity . . . all the right stuff. Made the best of a bad situation, turned his shit around. Earned everybody's respect on the inside. On the outside, too. He's the son of Angelo the Jet, a revered figure whose status in the Italian community dates back to his family being one of the original owners of Rao's restaurant. (In some circles, Angelo was also known as Angelo Cheesecake, which I guess was how Joey came by his Cupcake handle.) At the end of his stretch, Joey was pretty much beloved, by pretty much everyone in New York crime circles—all five families, and beyond.

It's impossible not to like this guy. He's got a big heart, a dynamic personality, comes across right away. I first met him when I went to visit Damon, late 1990s. Once Damon was out, I kept going to visit Joey. We became close—Blake and I had just been to a christening for his kid, so it's like we're a part of each other's family. He's like a brother to me.

So that's the setup.

The blowup started with a phone call from Joey's wife, Callie. Blake and I were in the car, Saturday morning, headed south on the Garden State to Atlantic City for a weekend with friends. We got an early start, left home by seven thirty, hoped to get down there and settled by late morning, enjoy the whole day. We'd had this weekend on the calendar for a while, been looking forward to it.

Poor Callie sounded frantic. "Ira, it's Joey. He's been in a fight."

I pressed her for details, but all Callie knew was that the guy on the other side of the fight had been hurt. How, she couldn't say. How badly, she couldn't say.

This was a problem. Joey was out on parole after a twenty-year haul. He knew better than to mix it up, no good reason. If this other guy was seriously hurt, it would go bad for Joey, even if it turned out to be self-defense.

Bottom line: you're on parole, you put a beating on a guy and it becomes a police matter . . . it's not good.

Callie told me Joey'd been taken to the Sixth Precinct, in the West Village. She kept saying, "What do I do, Ira? What do I do?"

First thing to do, I told her, was take a deep breath. "Relax, Callie. Let me make some calls. We don't know what we're dealing with until we know what we're dealing with."

I got Callie off the phone as soon as she calmed down, put in a call to Don't Worry Murray. He'd represented Joey for years.

"Murray, our friend's in trouble. Joey Cupcake."

"Joey? Aw, shit."

Just a couple days earlier, I'd been hanging with Murray at Joey's child's christening, the whole time Murray cracking jokes: "Can you believe this shit? All these guys and it's the two Jews with the most juice?" Like the two of us moving about on a kind of level playing field with some of the most powerful people in New York was the funniest thing in the fucking world.

Twenty minutes later, Murray called me back. By now it was about nine thirty in the morning, and Blake and I were a little more than halfway to Atlantic City—neither here nor there. We could turn around or press on, depending.

"Ira, it's bad."

"How bad?"

"Cops are saying guy's in a coma."

"Jesus, what happened?"

"Word is Joey beat him. Bad."

I thought, Shit. My mind raced ahead, tried to come up with some way Joey gets out of this the way he went in.

*Shit!*

Murray told me Joey was riding with two of his pals—let's call them Fast Eddie and Slow Sammy. I knew these guys, knew it was a bad mix. Fast Eddie did fifteen years. I remembered he had a temper. Slow Sammy—same thing.

"Murray, whatever you do, don't tell Callie," I said. "Let's get some details first."

If there's one thing I'd learned, my line of work, you don't rev up the wife—not until it's absolutely necessary.

Murray, his line of work said different. His line of work said to turn these guys into clients—something he was better at doing than any other criminal defense attorney in the city. So he reached back out to Callie, let her know he was on the case, let her know what was what, and now that she was all revved up, she was back on the phone with me.

"Your friend's a fuckin' asshole, Ira. He's still on parole, he goes off on this guy." Meaning Joey, not Murray.

"Relax, Callie. We don't know the whole story."

"He's got two kids, your asshole friend. He's a married man. Spent his whole childhood behind bars, and now he's out, he wants to throw it all away, land his ass back inside."

I was feeling the same way, thinking the same things, but I didn't say a word. I was pissed at Joey for putting himself in this spot, but I also had his back. It's like I was following some unwritten man-code—me, unable to talk shit about my friend to his wife, even if the shit was deserved.

Callie was agitated, anxious. I heard her kids screaming in the background. I heard another voice chiming in—all I know, one of her friends. It was like a madhouse, the other end of the phone.

I told Callie I'd call her back, got on the phone with the Sixth Precinct. I introduced myself, but I had no business there, no pull. I was just some asshole, calling about his asshole friend, telling the officer on duty I was a bondsman and hoping it might mean something. It did and it didn't. It got me a couple morsels of information instead of a runaround. I learned Joey and his pals had been brought in around three thirty in the morning. I learned the guy Joey beat up was not in a coma, after all. He was concussed, in bad shape, but he wasn't in a coma.

I called Callie back with this piece of news. "Thank God," she said.

I put it to her straight. "They're gonna violate him, Callie." Meaning, Joey would go down for a parole violation.

I didn't know the terms of Joey's parole. I seemed to remember he was out on a lifetime deal, but Callie set me straight, told me he only had a year and a half to go.

"He's not on life?" I asked. Making sure.

"No, thank God."

"Damn right, thank God. If he's on life, he's fucked, but if he's not, it might work out."

I ended the call and turned to Blake, shrugged, flashed her a look that said, *Hey, what are you gonna do?*

She'd been looking forward to this weekend, but she knew how things were with me and Joey. "Maybe we should just turn around, head home."

"We're not heading home," I said. Nothing I can do there anyway. It's Saturday morning, what the hell am I gonna do? Better to just work the phone.

So I worked the phone. I called a friend of mine, Norm, plugged into the city's database. I told him the story, asked if he could pull any information.

"Give me their names," he said.

"I just told you. Joey Cupcake, Fast Eddie, Slow Sammy."

"No, Ira. Their real names. Computer can't locate no Joey Cupcake."

Just then I realized, Fuck, I don't know their real names, so I made a quick call back to Callie, and she spelled them all out for me. Joseph Urgitano. Edward so-and-so. Sam so-and-so. I wrote them all down, made sure of the spelling, got things sorted out with Norm. He was on it. Called me back a couple minutes later. "Ira, there're three hundred and twenty-six people in the system."

It was a big number, but it covered all of New York City. My guys were about to be arraigned in Manhattan, through Central Booking. The way it works, so many people in the system waiting to be processed, a judge can usually hear eighty to ninety cases in an eight-hour shift. If he's jammed up and looking to clear the docket, he can maybe hear as many as a hundred—meaning, best case, they can process three hundred cases in a twenty-four-hour period, but there was no way to tell where Joey was in the queue. He could be called with the first group, he could be down at the bottom of the pile, in which case he wouldn't get to see the judge until Monday morning.

I got back on the phone with Norm. "Norm, you've got to do me a favor." Not really asking.

"What's that?"

"Can you jump him?" Meaning, find a way to get Joey's paper-work to the top of the pile.

Norm said he'd look into it.

Meanwhile, Blake and I pulled into the hotel—Revel, on the boardwalk. It was just after noon. We checked in, found our friends, got set up with a cabana. I ordered a couple drinks.

Blake saw me drinking. "How can you relax, Ira? You've got stuff going on."

"Who says I'm relaxed? I'm just drinking."

Norm called me back and told me I probably didn't want to jump Joey through early in the day.

"Why is that?"

"Judge on duty. You don't want him facing her." He gave me the name of a female judge, had it in for guys like Joey. Guys with a record, out on parole . . . she was by the book.

"No," I said. "Her we don't want. Who's on at night?"

He gave me the name of a judge we both thought might tilt a little more Joey's way—or, at least, might not go out of his way to jack him up.

"Can we push for this second shift, then?" I asked.

"You got it, Ira."

Six o'clock, I called Don't Worry Murray to tell him our paper-work was ready and Joey and his buddies were all set. But Mur-ray himself was not quite ready, hadn't figured on going down to court, thought he'd have his Saturday free. "How the hell did that happen?" he asked.

"I jumped them through the system."

"How?"

"Murr, I got my ways. Whoever you're sending down, get his ass over there."

And Murray did. Meanwhile, I got my guy Mike in my office to start putting together a bail package, just to be ready. Joey'd lost everything when he went away, but his parents left him a building in Harlem that was probably worth over a million, free and clear. I thought we could use the building to cover all three—Joey, Eddie, and Sammy. Assuming Eddie and Sammy even wanted to use me on this.

All these wheels were in motion back in New York—my office, Murray's office, Callie riding point from her cell phone at home—which meant there wasn't much for me to do down in Atlantic City but keep drinking. Just as we sat down to dinner, I got a call from Mike in my office, telling me the bails were set at $30,000, $25,000, and $10,000. The biggest number was for Joey. I was a little thrown by the low amounts, was thinking the bails would be ten times higher. With his record, Joey's bail could easily have been a buck fifty, two hundred, but I took this as a good sign. I took it to mean the judge saw the charges as more of a dustup than a game-changer.

By the time Mike got to court with the bail package, though, the place was shut down for the dinner break. This put the brakes on springing Joey anytime soon, but it didn't derail our celebration down in Atlantic City. The drinks kept coming. And coming. I was hammered, having a grand old time. I'd done what I could for my pal, and now I was just waiting for the bail hearing to play itself out.

Eleven o'clock at night, I was still waiting when a text came through from Mike, telling me the judge wouldn't sign our package.

I called back. "What do you mean, the judge won't sign?"

"He won't sign, Ira. Says he wants to see the property. Wants to call for a Nebbia hearing."

A Nebbia hearing, like a surety hearing, forces the defendant to demonstrate that the money for a bail comes from a legitimate source. In New York, this gives the judge up to seventy-two hours to examine the property and make sure it's legit, but I didn't see that it was warranted here. Typically, you'll see these types of hearings in a money-related case—an embezzlement charge, say, or maybe even a big drug charge. But this was an assault case, with three bails totaling $65,000—a number I could have covered without any collateral.

This made no sense to me, even hammered, and because I was hammered, it set me off. Felt to me like the judge was overstepping his authority, but I couldn't do a whole lot from Atlantic City.

I switched to drinking Red Bulls because I wanted to be sure I was awake, alert for whatever came next. We were still doing shots, but I chased each shot with caffeine, hoping the one canceled out the other.

By midnight, twelve thirty in the morning, the judges were leaving the bench. Things were looking grim for Joey Cupcake and his pals. I was starting to face the fact they wouldn't be released tonight—and since we'd already turned the corner into Sunday I was also starting to think they might not make it out by Monday.

It's like we'd gone from Plan A to Plan B, and then all the way through the whole damn alphabet.

Our buddies around the table at the restaurant in Atlantic City, they were all caught up in the drama, the excitement, but they didn't get the urgency. They'd seen enough cop shows, enough courtroom shows, they could kind of follow along. They could see I was scrambling, but that's where it ended for them. My buddy Rooster, he'd been following the story all damn day, he had a good sense of what I do, how the system works, and even he thought it was no big deal if these guys spent an extra night or two in jail. "I know they want to get home, Ira," he said. "But Joey's done twenty years. Fast Eddie, fifteen. So they're locked up another couple nights. What's the big deal?"

The big deal was, they'd nail Joey on a parole violation if we didn't clear him by Monday morning. The DA could have placed a parole hold on his paperwork in the beginning, but for whatever reason they didn't do that. A lot of times, parole officers aren't around over the weekend, so maybe the ADA on the case figured he'd let it slide for the time being. Whatever. But now that the judge had jacked us up on the bails, I needed to make sure Joey and his pals were released first thing Sunday, so I got Mike back on the phone, told him he needed to get down to the courthouse in the morning.

This was a problem. Mike coaches his daughter's Little League team, and they were playing in a tournament out on Long Island. Double elimination, first game starts at ten, so there was no way he was getting back to Manhattan in time to present our paperwork. This all came clear at about two thirty, three in the morning. Blake and I were up in our room, thinking about fooling around, but then my focus shifted. I couldn't ask Mike to miss out on his kid's tournament—me of all people. I live for this shit, know what it means to coach your kid, so now I was thinking we'd need to head out of here, bright and early, hustle back to the courthouse, handle this thing myself.

That's just what happened. We left word for our friends, didn't want to wake them, and checked out before breakfast, made good time back to New York. Poor Blake was exhausted, but I was running on fumes—and, probably, those last few shots of Red Bull. We arrived during the lunch break, so we ducked into Forlini's, on Baxter Street, a popular Italian joint for all the judges and lawyers working the courthouse. Place was empty, which I guess made sense. It was Sunday afternoon, early for any kind of lunch rush, so we sat down and looked at some menus. Just then, in walked the judge I was trying to avoid the day before—the Honorable Renee A. White. I knew Judge White would be back on the bench this afternoon, knew there'd be no avoiding her, so it's not like this was a total surprise, seeing her here. And it's not like it was such a terrible turn of events, her presiding. She's tough, but fair—and she'd always been good to me. Always treated me right.

I leaned over to Blake, gestured toward the judge. "That's the judge we're going in front of. Judge White."

We were the only other customers in the restaurant, so Blake tried to look without looking. "She seems nice enough," Blake whispered. "What does she have against Joey?"

"Nothing against Joey, exactly. More like she won't look too favorably on his record, him being in violation of his parole."

For a beat or two, I thought about picking up the judge's tab, but I knew she wasn't the type to accept it. Might rub her the wrong way. Still, it felt to me like I should say something, since we were the only ones in the restaurant. Also, it'd give me a chance to explain my appearance. I was wearing pressed jeans, a button-down shirt, loafers—fine for a weekend away at an Atlantic City hotel, but a little underdressed for a court appearance.

Blake and I finished our meal before the judge was even served, so we walked past her table on our way out the door.

"Your Honor," I said. "So nice to see you."

She looked up from her meal, nodded. "Mr. Judelson."

I introduced Blake, then I apologized for the way I was dressed.

"There's no need to apologize, Mr. Judelson," she said, all proper.

"It's just, I'm on my way back from a short vacation. Wasn't really expecting to be in court today."

"Excuse me?"

I moved to explain. "Three of my friends, they're in a bit of trouble. I cut my vacation short so I can post their bonds. I'll be in your courtroom this afternoon."

At this, she looked at me like I just took a dump at the foot of her table. "Not dressed like that, you won't."

"Now what?" Blake asked, as soon as we stepped outside.

"Maybe these guys aren't meant to get out," I said. "Maybe it's fate, keeps jacking us up."

Blake didn't buy this, thought we'd come this far, ruined our vacation. It was like a quest, getting these guys out. She wasn't about to let me throw up my hands and give up on the job.

I was due in court at two thirty. It was now one forty-five. I had less than an hour—but it was a Sunday afternoon, and there weren't a whole lot of men's clothing stores to begin with, this part of town, let alone any that were open. I was out of options, had no play, but then I thought of my guy Yoshi, worked for me in my Brooklyn office. He was just across the bridge, could probably hustle over here with some clothes.

Happily, mercifully, Yoshi answered his phone. He wasn't doing anything, said he'd be happy to run over. He's a heavyset kid, built like me, said he had something in his closet that might just fit.

I flipped the phone closed and turned to Blake. "He's on his way."

Twenty minutes later, Yoshi showed up outside the criminal court with a $59.99 suit—still had the price tag on it. The jacket looked like it'd fit me just fine, but the pants were a size 34. I raced the clothes upstairs to the men's room and struggled to put them on. I barely made it into the pants, which almost ripped at the back. I couldn't button the top button. I had to sit ramrod straight, and when I stood, I had to pinch the pants closed. The jacket was an okay fit. Wasn't too sure about the shirt Yoshi brought along, so I decided to wear my own.

Court was backed up a little. Two forty-five, the clerk brought our paperwork to the bench, told Judge White there was a pending matter of three bail bonds.

The judge didn't even look up from her desk and dismissed the bonds: "I'm not signing them." Like she couldn't even be bothered.

I could hear her from where I was sitting. It wasn't a conversation for the record, for the courtroom—just a sidebar-type exchange, between the judge and the clerk of the court. But I could hear Judge White explain that there was no issue with the bonds, just an issue with the bondsman: "Mr. Judelson is wearing jeans in my courtroom."

Soon as I heard this, I stood and caught the clerk's attention. "I've taken care of that," I said, pointing to my clothes.

At this, the clerk turned to Judge White. "Your Honor, it seems Mr. Judelson has gone out and bought a suit."

Finally, the judge looked up from her papers and motioned for me to approach the bench. So I did—carefully, because I didn't want to split my pants.

Judge White looked me up and down. Then she made a motion with her hand, indicating that I should turn around, like a male model. So I did this, too—also carefully.

She stared at me for a good long while. For a beat or two, I started to think she might smile, but she wasn't the type to smile in the courtroom. She was all-business, and when she was finally satisfied with my little fashion show, she asked, "And how was your vacation, Mr. Judelson?" Almost like she was being playful.

"Fine, Your Honor. Thank you."

Then she banged her gavel, stamped and signed the papers—and, boom, the bonds were approved. All three of them. The judge didn't even look at the collateral, so before she could change her mind or decide that my cheap suit wasn't quite up to her menswear standards, I raced over to the jail, paid the dollar bails on each of these guys, and sent my clients home.

(The dollar bails were to cover an additional charge on each case—like Joey's parole violation, which got recorded in the system as credit for time served.)

How the story turned out, they hit Joey with a curfew violation—a one-year prison sentence. No big thing, given what he was facing. But as I write this, he's still dealing with the assault charges on the case. When the dust clears, at least he'll also get a suit out of the deal. Not just because I'd give the "suit off my back" to Joey, but because that cheap suit wasn't close to fitting me. Not being able to fit into those pants really shook me up. I got home that night, stepped on the scale, and cringed: 219. Hadn't weighed myself in just about forever. Hadn't realized I'd gotten so big, so I went on a diet. But Joey? The suit will fit him perfectly.

# 12

# Power

On some days, it works out that you draw your power from your clients—meaning, you get it by association. Meaning, you're protected because you've done business with someone big, someone important.

Other days, the power is earned. It's more active than passive, which means it has more to do with who you are than who you know.

However you come to it, however it comes to you, there are two kinds of power in the bail bond business: there's explicit, brute-force-type power, and then there's subtle, play-the-advantages-type power, and I've come to realize you need a little bit of both if you want to keep an edge.

It's how you recognize it, what you learn to do with it that counts.

Take Dupree "Turf" Harris. I first met Turf in 2002. He was the purported leader of the Blood-Vicelord faction known as Code Red, out of Brooklyn. Turf came out of the notorious Marcy Projects in Bedford-Stuyvesant, one of the most dangerous housing projects in the city. He used to claim he was a cousin of Jay Z, so he was like royalty in New York gang circles. Turf was in and out of jail more times than he could count, and I bailed him out so many times we developed a friendship. He'd send me his boys when they were jammed up, and if they couldn't put together a decent bail package, Turf would step in and help them out. Once, he put up a gold chain. I had no idea what the thing was worth, no time to get it appraised, but the thing was so fucking thick and heavy I figured it had to cost $80,000, easy, which more than covered the bail, so I accepted it as collateral.

Turf had a mouthful of gold teeth, which he was always flashing—the guy smiled so much around me I thought his head would crack open. But you don't get to be a head of the Bloods unless you're also a vicious motherfucker, so that steady smile could be deceiving. My people would tell me Turf would cut you just as soon as he'd clap you on the back and collect you in a hug. I had no idea when I first met him that the guy could say the word and have your heart pulled out on the street, or he could have your heart pulled out in jail, but this became clear soon enough—to where I realized that most of New York City's gang activity moved on Turf's command.

We used to sit and joke and fart around in my office. The guy had a great laugh. He'd tell me stories about his cousin, only he'd never say it was his cousin. He'd *refer* to Jay Z but never mentioned him by name, like it was understood this was who he was talking about. Like everyone knew the connection. Anyway, word on the street was that Turf was the reason nobody ever fucked with Jay Z. I can't say with any authority that this was the case, but it makes sense—I mean, Jay Z was one of the few rappers of his stature who never got involved in any of that East Coast–West Coast bullshit. As a kid, yeah, he got into his share of trouble in Bed-Stuy; as a kid he'd made some mistakes; but once he reached a certain level, once his cousin Turf reached a certain level, it's like nothing could touch him. Jay Z became a business, man—one of his lines. And Turf, he became a different kind of legend.

Turf would fill me in on what was going on in the projects, in the hood, on the inside, all around. And I'd let him know how his boys were doing—the ones who had to keep checking in with me, anyway. We swapped information, had each other's back. "Anybody fucks with you, Ira, let me know," he would say. He'd even take it one step further: "Any of *my* people fuck with you, let me know." I never forgot that he was a bad dude, but I always appreciate any help when it comes to collecting money and keeping safe, so we got along just fine. We had each other's back.

And he was good to his word—like the time one of his boys jumped on a $25,000 bail Turf had signed for. I reached out to Turf to make good on the bond, but couldn't get him on the phone. I found out later that he'd burned all his phones, was running from extortion and racketeering charges of his own. Wasn't like him to disappear, to leave me hanging on a bail, so my first thought was that something must have happened to him. Then I started to think he'd beat me out on this one, despite our friendship.

A couple weeks after that $25,000 bail went south, I got a knock on my office door. It was late, my guys had gone home for the night, so it was just me. I opened the door and there was this kid, couldn't have been more than fifteen, sixteen—a red bandanna wrapped around his forehead. (Red—the Bloods' colors.) The kid handed me a bag of cash, $25,000, said, "This is from my boss." Then he walked out.

Turf turned himself in soon after that, went to trial, and now he's serving thirty-seven years—extortion, gunrunning . . . every damn charge you can think of. We write each other. His letters are insightful, personal, funny as hell. And he's *still* got my back, even on the inside.

His protection came in handy a couple years back, when a bunch of gangbangers came into my Brooklyn office, talking shit. They came seeking help, but they were disrespectful and out of control. All this bravado and testosterone was in the room, and it was getting in the way of my business. My other clients, my staff . . . everyone was on edge. These kids were clearly Bloods, and when I couldn't get them under control, I took the lead asshole aside and said, "You a Blood?"

The kid looked at me like I was from some old folks' home. "I don't talk about my colors, man."

"You know Turf Harris?"

Soon as I dropped Turf's name, the kid went white. But then he got some of his bluster back. "Anyone can say a name. Don't mean nothing."

"That so?" I pulled an article down from my office wall, talking about how I'd helped Turf out on a bail. Then I dug out one of Turf's letters from prison. Showed them both to this kid, who saw right away I wasn't just dropping Turf's name. The kid's whole demeanor changed. He dropped his shoulders, his tone softened, his swagger disappeared.

"Anyone can say a name, huh?" I said more than asked.

The kid didn't say a word, just looked like he'd been punched in the stomach.

I *loved* that power, man. I loved that it came from a place of mutual respect. I was Turf's boy. He was my boy. We looked out for each other. Yes, the guy might have been a cold-blooded killer. Yes, he had an organization of more than three hundred people behind him, and each and every one of those people would do anything he asked—*anything*, without question. But I never saw Turf's vicious side. I heard about it, but never saw it. I only saw him as a kid from the projects, looking for an edge, holding on to what he'd managed to build.

Far as I was concerned, that was the beginning and the end of it. That was all that mattered. The guy had made a name for himself, a reputation, and then he spent the rest of his life living up to that name, that reputation. Even in prison.

Only other person I ever knew with that kind of power was my uncle Phil—but in my uncle's case there was no violence, no viciousness. His power was way more subtle, came from his ability to read people—because this is a business of reads, after all. You go by your gut a lot of the time. You learn to read people—same way I learned to read Turf Harris. Uncle Phil taught me that, got me thinking in terms of good bets, bad bets . . . good reads, bad reads. There's always a thin, uncertain line between safe and sorry, and Uncle Phil knew how to walk that line better than anyone.

Guess I should finish up on Uncle Phil's story, since it's all tied up in mine. He died in 2005, after a long illness. He was ninety-five years old, and a tough old bird. He didn't take shit from anybody, didn't suffer fools all that gladly, couldn't stand incompetence or inefficiency of any kind. But you wouldn't have known any of that to look at him. He wasn't exactly rough around the edges. The people he met, he treated them with kindness—at least until they gave him a reason not to—and I always thought that was a good way to be.

Toward the end of his life, when he stepped away from the business, when I set out on my own, he used to tell me how proud he was of the man I'd become. Meant the world to me to hear that. Means the world to me still to think back on it. I was one of his reads. He saw something in me, made a big bet on me, and it paid off—for both of us—and there's not a day goes by that I don't think of him, channel him in some way, take something he taught me and put it to work.

Here's an example: I have this argument with my insurance company all the time. I'll go to them with a seven-figure bail, and I'm eager to get it approved because of the big fee, but they're always looking for more collateral. "Hey, if the guy had another million in collateral, he wouldn't need us," I tell them. "He'd just take out a home equity loan."

Uncle Phil used to say, "Fuck the collateral. Meet the people."

Once, a woman came into my office with a watch, said it was eighteen-karat gold, worth about $20,000. I had no idea if this was true, so she brought me an appraisal, said pretty much the same thing. I could have bought an appraisal off the street myself, so I handed it right back to her, "Now go bring me a real appraisal."

I had no way to know if this appraisal was legit, but I could see from this woman's body language that she was trying to deceive me. It wasn't about the watch. It wasn't about the paperwork. It was how she kind of flinched, recoiled, when I challenged her on it—like she was trying to put one over on me. Clearly, I couldn't trust her—and then, the more we talked, it was clearer still. First she didn't speak English, then she did speak English. Then I listened in when she spoke in Spanish to her family. She didn't think I understood, but I heard enough.

(Also, most of my guys in the office speak a little Spanish, so I'll try to have them sit in and translate.)

It's amazing what you can pick up when someone thinks you're not paying attention, and here I picked up that this wasn't someone I wanted to do business with. That's all. The bail was only for $20,000. The watch probably came close to that, and she was also putting up a fair amount of cash, so one way to look at it was there wasn't a whole lot of risk. But another way to look at it was I didn't get a good feeling from this woman, so I passed—figured I'd let some other bondsman deal with her shit.

That same week I met with the family of a fourteen-year-old boy who'd been nailed for stealing an iPad. Bail was $10,000, only the kid's parents had nothing to put up as collateral . . . *nothing*. But I wrote the bond anyway, just for my 10 percent fee, because I could see in the parents' eyes that this kid would catch hell. I could see they were mortified. This dumb kid didn't have to worry about being sent to jail—he had to worry about his father. The old man was an ironworker, and he'd beat the living fuck out of this kid if he stepped out of line—so, absolutely, I did the bail.

Uncle Phil would tell me to read people's eyes, but a lot of times he could get a read on a potential client over the phone. When I'd go out to Jersey to meet him for lunch, I'd sit across from him at his desk, listening to him work these people over, *listening* for some kind of tell. He'd trust his bondsmen, his guys in the field, but ultimately it was Uncle Phil's business, and he ran it like a dictatorship.

End of the day, it was his call—his reputation, his call—and I used to sit across from him and think, Now *that's* power. . . .

After I was on the job awhile I did a bail for a guy named Lavelle, whose father used to partner with Nicky Barnes in the drug business. Best way I can introduce Lavelle and Nicky Barnes is through a movie that came out a while back called *American Gangster*, with Cuba Gooding Jr. and Denzel Washington. Cuba Gooding Jr. played Nicky Barnes and Denzel Washington played the big-time drug dealer Frank Lucas.

Between the two of them, Barnes and Lucas pretty much ran the heroin trade in Harlem, for real—and Lavelle actually called Barnes "Uncle Nicky," for real. Was never quite sure of the relationship, but they were close, and I mention this connection here only to set up Lavelle's story, to show how deeply connected he was to the Harlem drug scene. It was a part of him, in a deep way—a way he couldn't shake for trying, as this story will show.

Lavelle's family reached out to me on a murder case. Bail was $400,000. The family had property in Virginia worth about $250,000, which wasn't enough to cover me, so I told them the only way I'd consider writing the bond was if I could talk to Lavelle directly, get a sense of his character. I couldn't look him in the eye because he was in jail, but I could at least talk to him, maybe get some kind of feel.

I knew who he was. I did my due diligence, talked to my friends on the street, knew Lavelle ran one of the toughest wards at Rikers. He was housed in the OBCC facility—the Otis Bantum Correctional Center—which was a hotbed of gang activity, but Lavelle himself wasn't affiliated with any one gang. He was like a lone wolf. On the outside, he ran a lot of the drug activity in Harlem; on the inside, he still managed to call the shots, so I knew I was dealing with a forceful character.

Naturally, I was seduced by the big number, but I wasn't sure about this bail, going in. Had more questions than answers. I wanted the premium, but I didn't like the risk. One thing working in Lavelle's favor was the DA had him on a murder charge, but it had taken the court a year and a half to get to bail, which told me the case was weak. The other thing he had going was the persistence of his family. They kept calling and calling, pleading with me to do the bond.

Soon as I got this guy on the phone, I found myself leaning his way. He spoke with such a sweet, soft voice, sounded nothing like his reputation. Told me with great force and conviction he was innocent of this murder charge. He actually told me a little more than that, a little more than I needed to know: "I might have done some serious shit, Mr. Judelson, but this body's not mine." Meaning, he wanted me to know he was being completely honest. Meaning, he might be a murderer, might not, but he didn't do this particular murder, and he wasn't about to go down for a crime he didn't commit.

"Lavelle, there's not a lot of money here, this property in Virginia. If you run, I'm fucked."

"I'm not running, Mr. Judelson."

"No offense, but how do I know that?"

"Because I'm telling you. I'm not running. I've done some stupid things in my life, but I'm not an idiot. Already got four years in. They've got no case. Where am I gonna go?"

Let me tell you, Lavelle was a persuasive guy. Even with that sweet, singsong voice, you could hear that he was a powerful presence, a man of his word, so I decided to do the bail. He came to see me when he got out, and we connected. I was struck by his appearance. He's short, stocky, ripped, but he had a way of locking eyes and talking to you straight that I thought was impressive, and from that first meeting we developed a strong relationship.

He ended up beating the charges against him, just like he said he would. The DA had no case. Took two years for it to go to trial, and Lavelle checked in with me the whole time. He worked as a personal trainer for a while, then I helped him get a job in the bricklayers' union. He could've gone back to Harlem and picked up right where he'd left off, but he didn't want to go that way. He didn't want to hit the streets—to "sling," as he called it. He was done with that life, clean, and I admired him for it.

"I ain't going back that way, Ira," he'd always say. He'd also tell me he had my back. "You're stuck with me, man. You got me for life."

I went to his wedding. I celebrated with him at the birth of his twin girls. He came to my house for barbecues. And I loved that he had his shit together, that things were going so well for him.

But all of this is background for my Lavelle story, because several years into our friendship I needed to call on him for help. A well-known Harlem rapper came into my office, wanted to put up a $50,000 bond to bail out a cop. Told me a wild story about fake badges and drugs and rogue police officers, which meant there'd be a surety hearing, to see that the money was legit. Trouble was, this rapper had no real property, just a bunch of jewelry, shit I'd have a hard time getting appraised. The whole deal seemed like more trouble than it was worth.

I had no idea who this rapper was, but one of the guys in my office recognized him, and I heard my guy in the outer office blowing smoke the rapper's way: "Man, I listen to all your music." And "Your shit's great." That kind of thing.

A pane of bulletproof glass in my office separates the reception area from our back office, and as I came out to see what was up, I saw this rapper in the reception area, starting to get all agitated that my guy wasn't buzzing him through. He had his posse with him—a bunch of kids, it looked like—so I jumped right into it. "My man, don't know what the fuck your problem is, but if you don't respect this office, if you don't respect me, I ain't doing your bail."

The rapper, he wasn't used to being treated this way, so he went off. "Do you know who I am? Do you even fucking know who I am?"

"I've got no fucking idea who you are, and I don't care," I said, not backing down an inch.

Then, to strut, the dude pulled a red bandanna out of his pocket and waved it in the air, no doubt telling me he was Blood-affiliated.

Things escalated from there, to where this asshole flashed a gun—just opened his shirt or his jacket to make sure we all saw the barrel.

I thought, Fool move.

The shit was getting real. I even started wishing I hadn't left my gun on the other side of the partition (I have a carrier license—pretty much have to, what I do for a living). But somehow, I convinced this rapper and his boys to chill, and eventually they made to leave, saying shit on the way out like "We'll be back, mother-fuckers!"

My girl Yvette was working that day, and my first thought was to get her out of the office, just in case these idiots came back, looking for some kind of stupid revenge, or even just to make some stupid trouble. My next thought was to call Lavelle, see what he knew about this rapper and his crew. I hadn't spoken to Lavelle in almost a year, but when I got him on the phone, I shot through the pleasantries and cut right to it. I mentioned the name of the well-known Harlem rapper. "You know this cat?"

"Hell yeah, I know that fuck," he said in way that told me straight off he didn't think much of this guy. "What's he up to?"

I told him what the rapper was up to, asked if he was Blood-affiliated.

"Man, he ain't no fuckin' Blood. He thinks he's Blood, but he ain't nothing, man. Did that shit make a step to you?" Meaning, did he threaten me in any way?

"I had a beef with him, here in my office."

"You sure it was him?"

"Positive. Kid in my office, works for me, he listens to all his music."

"That case, you just sit tight and don't worry about it."

"He won't be back?"

"Not like that, he won't be back."

About an hour later, I got a call from a guy saying he was a buddy of Lavelle's. Said he wanted to make sure he had his facts straight. "The rapper, he stepped to you?"

"Yeah, he did."

Next day, the well-known Harlem rapper came back into my office, and it was like night and day. His entire demeanor had changed. He could have been a different person. He was all sugary and apologetic. "Mr. Judelson, man, I'm so, so sorry about yesterday. I was out of line. I'll understand if you don't want to do the bail."

I shook his hand, said it was no problem, said we were good. I never did that bail, though. The rogue cop never got out the door. No other bondsman in town would take on that kind of risk, so the rapper's outburst, his bad behavior, it cost him. Don't know that I would have ended up doing the bail either way, but it cost him.

My man Lavelle . . . he bailed me out of this one. Taught me that when you run Harlem, when the drug trade flows through you, when you're the absolute king shit and you've got all this power, doesn't matter if you walk away from it, start to live clean. It attaches to you, becomes a part of you.

I would be lying if I said the raw side of power doesn't get me off, but I get just as much satisfaction, probably more, when I can use what I've built to help someone out. Especially family.

Outside of my uncle Phil and my wife, Blake, my father-in-law was my biggest fan when I was starting out. We connected. No question, he was the most generous person I'd ever met—a *giver* in every sense of the word. If he had a dollar, it was yours . . . even if it was his last dollar.

Ours wasn't your typical father-in-law/son-in-law relationship, more like a father-son relationship. I don't mean to take anything away from my own father, who I love, but Mr. G and I were cut the same way. My father had no business mind—wasn't his thing. His ideas on money and career were conservative: *get a paycheck, a pension, insurance . . . you're all set*. My father-in-law was more of a risk-taker, a gambler. He'd earn a bunch of money, he'd try to parlay it into a bigger bunch of money. He hustled. He liked that I'd had a bunch of businesses when I started seeing Blake. And he didn't care that those businesses had all gone bust, because to him the big score, the big opportunity, was always just around the corner.

Trouble was, my father-in-law couldn't catch a break. His hustling never took him anywhere. When I came on the scene, he'd just lost his house to foreclosure. He was in the garment district, making no money. He worked as a jobber, but he couldn't land a steady supply of material to sell. Before that, he was in the meat business—made a ton of money, all through the 1980s . . . until he didn't. Raised his young family in a nice house . . . until he lost it.

The man was a born salesman, could sell anything on the way out, but he had a tough time bringing in enough goods to make a living. With him, it was all about hits and misses—and unfortunately, the misses started piling up.

When my own career started to go off, I tried to help him out. He used to come see me at my Queens office near tears because of how much he was scraping. Other times he'd come by all excited to tell me about some new gig, some new deal he had cooking. I'd be so pumped for him, but then it would fall through. Once, I hooked him up with a wiseguy friend who was able to get his hands on barrels and barrels of Calvin Klein underwear. It was a shady deal, but it was something, and my father-in-law grabbed at it. But then the wiseguy got whacked and we had no way to get the goods.

My father-in-law was my eyes and ears on the police beat. He listened to 1010 WINS all the time. He'd call me up, tell me there'd been a big mob bust, a big gang bust, a big SEC bust, tell me I should get on it. He had a good feel for my business, understood what I did in a way most "civilians" couldn't. For the longest time, I wanted him to come work for me, but Blake worried it would ruin our relationship, so I lent him money on the side. I set him up in all these different deals—in the limousine business, in the DirecTV business, in whatever opportunity he had cooking.

He came down with bladder cancer around the time Blake and I got married, but he beat it. He came to the wedding looking pretty banged up—but when he was first diagnosed, no one thought he'd even make it to the wedding, so it was a good trade. You look like shit, but you're still here—you'll take that. He got his legs back after that, started feeling better, stronger, but as he got his health back, he started to lose his way in business. Don't know that the one had anything to do with the other, but it was like another trade, you swap out one struggle for another.

Jump ahead ten years or so, New Year's Eve. My in-laws came over to babysit so Blake and I could go out. We were home by twelve thirty, and soon as we walked in the door, my mother-in-law huddled with Blake to tell her she was worried about her father. "He's been coughing all night."

I sidled over to Mr. G—even after Blake and I were married, I called him Mr. G—and asked him if he felt all right.

"I'm okay. It's just this cough."

"Tomorrow, you'll go to the doctor, get it checked out."

He wasn't much for doctors, my father-in-law. For one thing, his health insurance wasn't great, so he worried how he'd pay for an office visit, but I told him I'd take care of it. Told him I'd even make the appointment.

The doctor said he had pneumonia, put him on antibiotics, but three weeks later my father-in-law was still coughing. He lost a ton of weight, looked like hell. Each day, he seemed to get worse, so he went back to the doctor. This time, they put him on a heavier dose of antibiotics, still thought it was pneumonia.

A couple weeks later, same thing. He stopped by to see me at my Queens office one afternoon, and he could barely breathe. He was driving his limo in those days, had an airport fare, swung by to say hello, but he was dragging. He couldn't get two words out without gasping for air, so I rushed him over to North Shore Hospital, out on Long Island. I called Blake on the way, told her to tell her mother and brother to meet us there.

They ended up admitting him—for observation, they said. Nobody could say for sure what was wrong with him, so they ran a series of tests on him and the results weren't good. Our worst fears realized. A doctor came by and spoke to us in the waiting area. "He has cancer."

Our first thought was that this was the bladder cancer, back from remission, but this time it was lung cancer. My father-in-law had been a big-time smoker most of his life. He managed to stop when he was diagnosed with bladder cancer, but now this doctor was telling us they could do nothing for him.

"Take him home," he said.

We heard those words—*take him home*—like a kick to the stomach. Like a death sentence. Blake, her mother, her brother, me . . . we went from shell-shocked to grieving to ripshit in about ten seconds. I was so mad, I started yelling at the doctor. "What the fuck do you mean, take him home?"

They brought in another doctor to calm us down, and this one patiently explained that the cancer had metastasized. He said my father-in-law had maybe three weeks to live, said they could do nothing for him at the hospital, said he'd be more comfortable in his own bed. He even said the hospital could recommend some sort of home hospice setup, so within just a few hours we went from thinking there was this nagging cough, this lingering pneumonia, to talking about final days.

Blake was hysterical. We were all upset, crying, fuming. Plus, the doctors were telling us there were no cancer beds for my father-in-law at any of the top hospitals in the city, and reminding us that they could do nothing for him anyway at North Shore, so they were kind of throwing up their hands. They said they'd reach out to other hospitals in the area, but they didn't sound too hopeful—or too helpful.

I'm always thinking there's someone I can call, some end-around maneuver I can pull to get what I want, what I need. To make something happen. So I started working the phones. First call I made was to a rabbi I'd done a big bail for in Park Slope—the guy knew practically everyone there was to know in New York City.

No, this wasn't the same rabbi I'd bailed out in time for Passover—Rabbi Baruch Lebovits—but I guess you could say I'm the bondsman of choice for Park Slope rabbis. Don't know why I thought this guy could help, but I remembered that he was an important player, had a ton of influence, friends in high places.

"Rabbi, my father-in-law is very, very sick," I said. "Cancer. The doctors here say there's nothing they can do for him."

"Ira, where are you now?"

"North Shore Hospital."

"Stay there. I will call you right back."

Second call was to Tony. Like the rabbi, Tony also had the city wired, but with his own set of *family* connections. The problem was to find a bed in one of the city's top cancer hospitals—and along with the bed, a doctor to take over my father-in-law's care. Blake's brother was a dentist, working out of North Shore Hos pital, but he wasn't getting anywhere with his doctor friends and associates on Long Island. And Blake and her mom knew some people to call, but no one was coming through for us.

Tony went to work trying to get us a bed at Sloan-Kettering, and the rabbi set his sights on NYU. The rabbi struck first—said he could get my father-in-law a bed *and* an appointment with Dr. Abraham Chachoua, who was the best lung doctor in the city.

"You have to take this appointment, Ira," the rabbi said. "This is the guy your father-in-law needs."

We got Dr. Chachoua on the phone and filled him in.

"You're a friend of the rebbe?" he asked.

"Yes," I said.

"Then get him over here right away. I'll have a bed for him."

It had been a couple hours since the doctor came into the waiting area to give us this grim diagnosis, and we still hadn't told my father-in-law the full story. We didn't want his spirits to sag, so Blake and her mother took turns sitting with him while her brother and I stayed in the hallway, working the phones. We'd been at the hospital seven or eight hours, it was pushing midnight, we were all thrashed—emotionally and physically. Don't think any of us was thinking too, too clearly.

The next problem was with my father-in-law's paperwork. The hospital wouldn't discharge him at first, which made no fucking sense to me. Here they were telling us they could do nothing for him, telling us to take him home, but they wouldn't let us leave. We had a top doctor waiting for him in the city, a bed at a top hospital, and these idiots were dragging their feet on Long Island.

Without the hospital's help, it was tough to arrange for transportation to the city, because it's not like we could have thrown my father-in-law in the back of our car and driven him ourselves.

I mean, we *could* have, but he was in bad shape, getting all these fluids intravenously, so I called a buddy of mine named Kuku, who ran an ambulette company.

"Kuku, I need a favor."

"When and where?" were his exact words.

The ambulette was there in less than an hour, and the hospital still wouldn't release him, so we just kind of wheeled him out of there against medical advice. The poor guy could hardly move, could hardly breathe. He was so sick. We got him to NYU at about three o'clock in the morning, got him settled in. We were with him the whole time. Finally, around six, Dr. Chachoua came by to examine him, go over his chart, so we all stepped out of the room and let the doctor do his thing.

After a while, Dr. Chachoua came out into the hallway to talk to us. He gave it to us straight—said the cancer had spread to both lungs, said it might have spread to the brain. He scheduled an MRI for later that morning, then he told us how he liked to treat this type of cancer. He was aggressive, he said. He liked to give his patients what he called a "crazy, mixed-up cocktail"—a chemo-cocktail, obviously—and he'd had some success with this approach.

"At North Shore, they gave us three weeks," Blake said.

"I won't lie to you. He's very, very sick," the doctor said. "But I think we can beat that."

Blake was suddenly hopeful, thought she'd heard him say something else. "Beat the cancer?"

"No, I can't say that. I don't think I can save him," the doctor said. "But I can certainly buy him some time."

Whatever Dr. Chachoua could do for my father-in-law, whatever he couldn't, it sounded a whole lot more promising than three weeks.

Finally, we went back to the room and told my father-in-law what was going on. I think he must have known, but this was the first time we talked about the cancer in front of him. This was the first time he heard about the North Shore doctor's prognosis. Dr. Chachoua came with us to tell Mr. G about his treatment and to answer any questions he might have.

Blake took her father's hand and said, "We need you to fight."

"Fine. I'll fight," my father-in-law said.

The rabbi came by to see how we were doing—he even asked to sit with my father-in-law for a while. To this day, I've got no idea what those two talked about, but every time the rabbi's name came up afterward my father-in-law would smile and say, "Hey, I love that guy!"

Later that same morning, Tony called. He'd gotten a bed for my father-in-law at Sloan-Kettering, but we'd thrown in with Dr. Chachoua. It made no sense to think about moving my father-in-law or switching up his care.

And Dr. Chachoua's crazy cocktail seemed to work. The tumors in the lungs began to shrink. My father-in-law started to feel better, more like himself. He even went back to work. That three-week death sentence he'd been given at North Shore Hospital? He shot right past it and just kept going. He was going great guns until one day about six months into his treatment he caught a cold. And that was that. It's like a light switch went off, just from this one lousy cold.

By the next day he was gone. But we bought ourselves a bunch of time . . . and I came away thinking it's not what you know that counts. It's not even *who* you know. It's how you push the buttons and work the angles and fix the problems.

# EPILOGUE

## The Perfect Day

I don't have time to sit and think about my life in full. Can't imagine anyone with kids and a demanding job has any kind of easier time of it, but I can only speak to my own experience. I can only admit that I'm all-out, all the time—there's just no way to take an objective view. But I do know this: it's an absolute fucking blast, the bail bond business. One giant adrenaline rush after another.

Wouldn't change it for the world.

That said, I sometimes think I'm the last of a dying breed. Oh, there'll always be bondsmen like myself, long as there are bad guys caught in the system, but the nature of my business is bound to change. Already, it's changing. Haven't even been at it for twenty years, and it's upside down and bent in ways my uncle

Phil could never have imagined. Part of that is the technology—it's now possible to track the twists and turns of every case with just a couple keystrokes on the computer. Part of that is the *politically correct* world we now live in—it's gotten to where a hardworking, heart-in-the-right-place bondsman can't cut a couple corners without worrying he'll lose his license. Judges, attorneys, media types . . . everyone's so focused on walking a safe, straight line, there's less and less opportunity to shake things up or go at these cases in a brand-new way. Plus, the young guys coming in are slicker than I ever was—slicker than I ever want to be. (If you ever catch me coming at a case from a place of poise and polish, feel free to smack me around.) (Oh, and one more thing: if you ever hear that I'm not out to help my clients, to fight for them, make their bids go easy, I hope you'll call me on it—and smack me around some more.) These kid bondsmen, they don't read people the way Uncle Phil taught me to read people. Instead, they look at spreadsheets and assess risk in ways that have nothing to do with *feel*. They listen to their head instead of their heart. They shy away from doing a bond if it looks like it'll be too much hassle.

But with me it's always been about the hassle. Sometimes, the hassle has been the best part. The hassle . . . the hustle . . . the raw, relentless thrill . . . it all ties in.

Hey, if this shit was easy and straightforward, anyone could do it. And it wouldn't be any fun.

*One* story kind of ties it all together, gets close to how things are with me at work, at home, all around. It's got it all, this one, and it starts with a guy who had one of the biggest hit records of all time. . . .

•    •    •

Joseph Brooks was a songwriter, screenwriter, and producer—probably best known for writing "You Light Up My Life." He was also a dark character. In June 2009, he was indicted on ninety-one counts of rape, sexual-abuse, and assault charges—allegedly, his thing was to lure aspiring actresses to his New York City apartment with the promise of an audition, which he would turn into a sick, twisted scene.

He was out on a $500,000 cash bail when I was called in by his lawyer, after an additional set of victims came forward to testify against this asshole. This meant the DA could build a whole new case, with a whole new set of charges, and Brooks was taken back into custody. The attorney thought it would be helpful to bring in a bondsman to put a bail package together, to see if the client could get out the door using that initial $500,000 bail as a down payment.

Brooks looked like the devil—dark eyes, drawn face, an empty, hollow demeanor. He oozed creepiness, this guy. Wasn't for me to say he deserved to walk the streets, but if the judge put some kind of doable number on his freedom, I had no problem posting the bond. Brooks had money, that wasn't an issue. He had property. So I went to see the judge to get his take.

"Judge, the lawyer wants me involved. What's it look like to you?"

The judge shared his thinking, off the record.

"My kids need to eat," I said. Like I needed to explain my interest, bailing out such a creepy, despicable character. Like I hadn't already worked this line into the ground with every judge in town.

The judge laughed. "Then you should do fine on this one."

Bail was ultimately set at $1.25 million, but the judge kept the

$500,000 in place and added another $750,000. He could have exonerated the first bail and made it a full, flat $1.25 million, but that would have cost Brooks the corresponding fees, which at these amounts came to a lot of money. The judge also wanted an ankle bracelet, so I went to work on the bail package, reached out to another of my bracelet guys to set the whole thing up—this time, through a monitoring company I worked with in North Carolina.

For about a year, Brooks was a good soldier and checked in when he was supposed to. Make no mistake, he was a slimy guy, but he did what he was told, gave me no reason to think he'd jump.

Until he did.

First sign of trouble was also the last. I was coaching Casey's Little League team, final game of the season, and I want to offer fair warning here because the rest of this story played out like a movie of the week—but, hey, you can't make this shit up.

A little background on this Little League season: We started out the year like the Bad News Bears, ended up playing like the Yankees. This last game was symbolic. We'd played this same team, first game of the year, and they beat us 25–0. Only reason I remembered such a miserable score was because the league played with a 5-run mercy rule; you could only score 5 runs in an inning before your side was "retired" and the other team was allowed to take their licks. Games were seven innings, but if you were up by double digits after five innings, the game was called—I guess so the kids on the losing team didn't have to look at the scoreboard to remind themselves they'd gotten the shit kicked out of them.

So it was the bottom of the seventh, last game, and Casey's team was down only 14–11. Wasn't exactly the league championship, but in our heads the game had that kind of weight. I'd tried to get the kids thinking about it like a statement game, a chance to show the other kids in the league how much we'd improved, to end the season on a high note.

We loaded the bases and pushed across a run to make the score 14–12, and Casey came to the plate with the bases still full. He went into all of his little at-bat rituals he practiced in our backyard—you know, banging the dirt from his cleats with his bat, taking his last few practice swings . . . trying to look like his favorite ballplayers. It was a big-time moment—not just for Casey, but for me, too. I lived for this kind of stuff, for these moments on the ball field with my children. I was coaching third base, which was where I always put myself, thought it was the best place for me to communicate with the kids while we were up at bat, so I was hollering instructions out to our base runners, making sure they knew the situation—hollering out at Casey to wait for his pitch, keep his eye on the ball . . . all of that.

Just then my phone started vibrating. Couldn't have happened at a worse time. I stole a peak, but kept my eyes on the game. I recognized the number as a North Carolina area code, couldn't think who'd be calling me from North Carolina, so I fisted the phone back in my pocket and turned my attention back to Casey. This was a big spot, and I was pulling for him like crazy. The opposing coach came out to talk to his pitcher, so Casey kind of hung back for a bit, kicked some more dirt from his cleats, and then the phone vibrated again. This time it was a text message from the same number, telling me the bracelet on Joseph Brooks had been tampered with.

My first thought was, Shit! That's $750,000 if this guy's jumped.

My second thought was, Shit! Casey's up, in a big spot, making like he's Derek Jeter in the on-deck circle while the opposing pitcher gets a talking-to, and here I am looking at my cell phone, worrying about work.

Either way I was fucked.

Blake saw what was going on right away, flashed me this look that told me I was deep in her doghouse just for looking at my phone. I sent her back more of a shrug than a look, meant to tell her there was nothing I could do.

I called over to my friend Adam, my assistant coach, asked him to cover third base for me while I stepped away from the field to check in with the monitoring company.

Blake jumped down from the bleachers to intercept me. "What the fuck are you doing, Ira?"

She knew exactly what the fuck I was doing, so I didn't exactly appreciate the question, but I owed her an answer. "It's my bail, Blake. It's a lot of money. What the fuck do you want me to do?"

"I want you to be here for your son. It's a Saturday afternoon." Then she marched back to her spot in the stands and cheered a little extra loudly for Casey; felt to me like she was rubbing it in.

I had no numbers for Brooks in my cell phone, so I called my guy Winston at the office. "Joseph Brooks, the detective on the case, what's his number?"

"Who?"

"Look under the big bonds, Joseph Brooks. Three-quarters of a million," I said.

While Winston looked up the file, I watched Casey step to the plate, start to work the count in his favor. I covered the mouthpiece of the phone and called out to him from behind the fence, "Wait for your pitch, Case!"

It was something to say—a way to put it out there to Blake that I was still in the moment.

I got the number, dialed, waited for the call to go through while Casey was still waiting for his pitch. I knew I'd catch hell from Blake when we got home, but I didn't think I had any choice but to follow up on this bail. Little League was Little League. Business was business. A lot of dads had to miss one for the other, and this was me on the wrong side of the equation.

I finally got the detective on the line, told him why I was calling. "What's going on with Joseph Brooks?"

"Who are you?"

"Ira Judelson, I'm the bondsman."

"The bondsman?" He repeated it like he'd never heard of such a thing, had no idea why he should talk to me on this.

"I wrote Mr. Brooks's bond. I need to know if the bond is okay."

The cop didn't respond at first, then finally said, "You're fine. Your bond is okay." It sounded to me like he was speaking cryptically, holding something back.

"What does that mean? Is there a problem?" Not letting him off the hook.

There was another pause, and in the space between my question and the detective's delayed response, I heard the crack of Casey's bat, turned, and saw he'd hit a hard ground ball to the right side of the infield. The folks in the stands jumped to their feet, and I broke toward the field just as the cop started to answer.

"All I can say is your bond is safe, Mr. Judelson."

The ball skidded into right field, just beyond the second baseman's reach, and our base runners started circling the bases like they were on a merry-go-round. My buddy Adam was jumping up and down in the third-base coaching box, waving the runners home, while I stopped just short of the field as the second runner came around to score, tying the game at 14–14.

I jumped, hooped, hollered, swept up in the moment, thrilled for Casey, thrilled for the team, but at the same time I was stuck on this phone call, on what wasn't being said, so between screams and cheers I tried to pull some more information from this detective.

"What does that mean, 'your bond is safe'? That mean he's dead? Is Mr. Brooks dead?"

The right fielder had a tough time getting the ball back into the infield, so the kid who'd been on first came home to score the winning run, and just as he crossed the plate, the cop said, "Yes. I can't tell you anything more, but yes."

I let out an adrenaline whoop of joy, pumped my fist into the air in celebration, and ran toward the pile of kids at home plate, jumping up and down like they'd just won the World Series. Just before I got there, I finished up the call with the detective: "Thanks." Snapped the phone shut, thought briefly the guy might have mistaken my adrenaline-whoop as me celebrating Joseph Brooks's death, when it wasn't that way at all.

As moments go, this one was pretty damn great. I was over the moon for Casey, but I hated that I'd had to separate myself and step away from third base and make those couple calls to chase my bond. I sought out Casey in the scrum of kids and picked him up in the air, squeezed him tight, told him how proud I was of him, how much I loved him, but underneath all of this good stuff I couldn't shake thinking I'd cheated him out of a small piece of this pretty damn great moment. And mostly, that I'd cheated my-self out of it.

But it was all good. My kid won the game with a walk-off double—that's how it goes down in the memory books, as a game-winning, bases-clearing rope down the right-field line.

And my $750,000 bond was intact—another something for the memory books.

Later that afternoon, I learned the full story of what happened to Joseph Brooks. He was found dead in his apartment with a plastic bag over his head, a helium tank and a hose at his feet, a suicide note on the table. Apparently, when the EMT guys were called to the apartment, they cut off the bracelet, had no idea what it was, and that's what set off the alert with the bracelet company.

I never did get that bracelet back. I had to pay to replace it—didn't have it in me to go after the Brooks estate to reimburse me—but I counted it a small price to pay for getting off that bond, for seeing my kid get the thrill of his little lifetime.

For having it all—my version of it, anyway.

# ACKNOWLEDGMENTS

I've been blessed with some wonderful people in my life who've set me up and propped me up and picked me up—whenever I was down. First, I'm grateful to my uncle Phil Konvitz, who bailed me out of some serious shit and gave me my start in the bond business. For a man who might not have stood so tall, he carried such weight and class and power.

I'm indebted, too, to my in-laws—Noel and Lois Gardner— but for different reasons. My late father-in-law, Noel, was one of my earliest supporters. To this day, I give my mother-in-law grief for trying to fix her daughter up with a doctor or a lawyer— *even after we were engaged!* But Noel saw something in me— and, soon enough, Lois did, too. Without their love and support, I don't know how Blake and I would have made it through when we were just starting out.

My parents, Edward and Arlene Judelson, are deserving of great thanks as well. I know I give my father a hard time in these pages—mostly for giving me a hard time when I was younger— but at the end of the day he and my mom were always there for me, no questions asked. They gave me the core set of values I carry with me on the streets every single day. Who I am, what I'm about—it goes back to them.

## ACKNOWLEDGMENTS

My brother, Barry, also rates a mention here. We had the usual sibling rivalry–type issues growing up, but as adults we've become more than just brothers. We're actually friends, and I'm grateful for his love and support—and for the way he keeps me honest.

On the book front, I want to thank Jay Mandel at William Morris Endeavor, for helping to get this project off the ground, and his colleague Mel Berger, for putting me in touch with my cowriter, Daniel Paisner. If this book sounds like me, smells like me, *feels* like me, it's because of Dan's ability to capture my voice and get to the heart of what I do for a living, how I do it, and who I do it with. Thanks, Dan, for bringing it all across.

Our editor, Matthew Benjamin, has been a tireless champion of this book from the very beginning. His instincts have helped to make this book better, tighter, richer—and I appreciate his extra efforts. And, I'm grateful for the dedication of his Touchstone colleagues as well. Thank you!

And finally, on the homefront, a special shout-out to my children—Ava, Casey, and Charlie. I work hard enough as it is, and this book pulled me away from you even more. I'm sorry about that, just as I'm sorry that the work I do can seem scary and confusing to you at times. So thank you for your patience, and your understanding, and your great strength. Everything I do, I do for you. I love you, guys.

# ABOUT THE AUTHORS

**IRA JUDELSON** is one of New York's most prominent bail bondsmen. For nearly twenty years, he has posted bail for dozens of the city's most notorious defendant-celebrities, including athletes, hip-hop artists, moguls, and media personalities, as well as thousands of common (and not-so-common) criminals. He is well known to defense attorneys, judges, court officials, and reporters for his no-nonsense demeanor, his charismatic charm, and his ability to "read" a prospective client. He lives in Westchester, New York, with his wife and three children. Read more about him at www .irajudelsonbailbonds.com.

**DANIEL PAISNER** is the author of more than fifty books, on topics ranging from business and sports to politics and entertainment. He is also one of the busiest collaborators in publishing, having had a hand in the autobiographies and memoirs of some of our best-known athletes, actors, politicians, television personalities, and "ordinary" individuals who have conquered extraordinary situations.